RAVE REVIEWS FROM ALL OVER FOR THE PHENOMENAL #1 BESTSELLER...

o   o   o

"THERE'S NO WAY IN THE WORLD YOU CAN GO WRONG WITH GRETZKY. THE GREAT ONE STRIKES AGAIN."
Toronto Sun

o   o

"THERE IS A LOT OF FRESH AND REFRESHING MATERIAL. An absolute gem of a chapter is titled 'Yours Truly.' In this chapter you get to know Gretzky better than ever. The book is bright and breezy with a style as slick as Gretzky has on the ice. It's an absolute must."
Edmonton Sun

"THE GRETZKY WE SEE HERE ISN'T ALWAYS THE HUMBLE, AW-SHUCKS GUY YOU SEE ON TV.

"The best parts come in the chapter titled 'Yours Truly,' in which Gretzky theorizes on what makes him hockey's foremost creative wizard. The key things, he says, are anticipation and constantly applying intelligence to find new approaches that place him a step ahead of all the others. These simple secrets were passed down by father Walter, who gave Wayne his first skates when Wayne was 2, drilled maxims such as "Skate to where the puck's going and not where it's been" into his brain, and then told him to find new tricks."

The Globe and Mail [Toronto]

○   ○   ○

"MY ADVICE: BUY THIS BOOK, ENJOY IT. It's a fun book, a family book, a story King Arthur and his round table of knights would be proud of. The nice young man scores again."

The London Free Press

○   ○   ○

"HE WRITES, HE SCORES. Gretzky: An Autobi-

ography *shows what true champions are made of. It will be essential reading for a few million kids—and maybe, just maybe, might inspire one or two of them to someday be as great as Gretzky."*

Calgary Herald

○   ○   ○

"IT'S AN INTERESTING STORY. *In a chapter titled 'The Day I Made Transactions,' Gretzky tells exactly how the trade to Los Angeles happened. The story does not flatter Pocklington.*

"The book explains why Gretzky and Sather had their differences and portrays Pocklington as a liar who dumped Gretzky to bail out his struggling business interests."

The Vancouver Province

○   ○   ○

"GRETZKY DOESN'T DISAPPOINT. *He pulls no punches when talking about Oiler owner Peter Pocklington, who is portrayed as petty and cheap. By now the true story about the trade is known, but Gretzky's side of it still makes good reading. We also learn a lot about what it's like to be so famous. Sometimes it's funny (he says 'Tu es tres belle' to a beautiful young woman in a Montreal mall and she faints); sometimes it's* not *(he won't go out alone because he's afraid of getting knifed). For people who play the game, the best part of the book may be the fascinating discussion of his hockey talent. 'If you ask a fifty-goal scorer what the goalie looks like, he'll say the goalie's just a blur,' he writes. 'But if you ask a five-goal scorer, he'll say the goalie looks like a huge glob of pads. A five-goal scorer can tell you the brand name of the pads of every goalie in the league.'"*

Quill & Quire

o   o   o

"FOR A HOCKEY FAN, IT'S THE NEXT BEST THING TO WATCHING THE GREAT ONE WORK HIS MAGIC ON THE ICE.

"This is a rarity among modern sports autobiographies. Gretzky isn't out to stroke his own ego or slam his foes into the boards—although he does take a couple of runs at Pocklington. He has a story to tell and he does it with surprising wit and the same fluency he displays on the ice."

The Telegraph-Journal [Halifax]

o   o   o

"WAYNE GRETZKY IS NOT ONLY AN UNFORGETTABLE PLAYER, HE'S ALSO AN INSATIABLE FAN; AND THAT'S WHAT MAKES HIS BOOK SO SATISFYING. *He* knows what we really want to know about is the kicks—big and small—he gets from a game he's refined to the smoothest possible finish on and off the ice.

"But he's no wimp. And for those who can't read between the lines, he spells everything out in a 10-point plan to revamp the league."

Books in Canada

o   o   o

"GRETZKY COMES ACROSS AS HAVING AN INSATIABLE LOVE OF THE GAME, AND A BRILLIANT INSIGHT INTO HOW IT SHOULD BE PLAYED. With simple tact, Wayne displays great respect for opponents, the less fortunate, and even the people who have orchestrated the low points—few but intense—in this life.

"This book has given Gretzky the opportunity to say what he meant all those times he was caught out of breath in some foreign arena. He has made good use of it."

Halifax Chronicle Herald

GRETZKY

An Autobiography

GRETZKY

An Autobiography

Wayne Gretzky

with Rick Reilly

HarperCollins*Publishers*
Toronto

Credits for photo inserts follow the index.

First published 1990 by HarperCollins Publishers Ltd.
First paperback edition published 1991

Typesetting by Harold Hill & Co.

Canadian Cataloguing-in-Publication Data

Gretzky, Wayne, 1961—
    Gretzky : an autobiography

ISBN 0-00-637742-4

    1. Gretzky, Wayne, 1961— . 2. Hockey players — Canada — Biogra-
phy. I. Reilly, Rick. II. Title.
GV848.5.G73A3 1991   796.962'092   C91-093904-7
[B]   89-46532

    91 92 93 94   OFF   10 9 8 7 6 5 4 3 2 1

Contents

Preface

My back was killing me, we'd just been hammered in Game Five of our playoff series with the Calgary Flames, it had been a miserable season, and we still had two hours left on a three-hour flight. But I was feeling just fine.

I was thinking about the last couple of years of my life. I was thinking of the people who thought I was crazy to have agreed to a trade that sent me from one of the greatest dynasties in National Hockey League history to a team that hadn't won a title in twenty-two seasons. They didn't know what *really* happened when I left the Edmonton Oilers. And I don't think they knew much about what motivates athletes and what builds great teams either.

We were flying back on the 727 our owner, Bruce McNall, bought to make our lives easier. Travel is the worst part of the professional athlete's life. Flight after flight, often at night. Departure delays, lousy food. My bags are *where?* But on our team plane, every seat is first class, all sixty of them. And there's four different kinds of Häagen-Dazs waiting.

Every four or five banks of seats there's a monitor for watching videos of a game — or a film — and Bruce has already made plans to add a complete high-tech video room so the coaches can edit and study tapes, and a massage room in the back for our team masseur, Jurgin, to give treatments.

But it's not the plane. It's why Bruce thought of it, how he handles things. Unlike the Oilers' owner, Peter Pocklington, McNall doesn't depend on the Kings financially. Bruce is an NHL owner largely because he loves hockey. Peter Pocklington worried about nothing but the bottom line. Bruce McNall worries about the next day's box score. He's a fan, he wants to see the team improve, and he doesn't seem to care how deep he has to dig into his pockets to be sure it happens.

That's why he got that plane. We didn't need to have one. How many other teams in pro sports have their own plane? Not many, and no other team in the NHL. Some people criticize Bruce's extravagance. But if the Montreal Canadiens are playing us in Los Angeles on Monday night, they'll fly all day Tuesday and be home late Tuesday night. They've blown a day of practice and their practice on Wednesday will probably be lousy because everybody's so burnt out from the traveling. Whereas if we're in Montreal on Monday night, we're back in our beds in L.A. that same night because of the time change. Now we take all of Tuesday off to rest and our practice Wednesday is a great one. On top of that Bruce has saved a night's hotel charges for fifty-some people. It might only win you four or five games a year, but four or five more wins a year might get you the home edge during the playoffs, and home edge during the playoffs might just get you a piece of the Stanley Cup.

Not that it was always like this with the Los Angeles Kings. I remember when I came to my first Kings training camp in September 1988. Bruce had been the owner for only a few months. I could tell right away that this team had become comfortable with losing. You could feel it, even though my first day was a media circus. Our camp was off the beaten track in Victoria in British Columbia, but the ice was jammed with photographers wanting to catch my first day as an L.A. King. I had been nervous about this.

The trade had gotten more publicity than I ever dreamed it would, and I didn't want anyone to think I was walking into camp like I owned the place. I had wanted to low-key it, to keep quiet and not make anybody uncomfortable, but the media were acting like it was Game Seven of the Stanley Cup. This was not good.

Then something happened to put me totally at ease. Mike Allison, a center, walked up to me, held out his hand and said, "Well, they finally got someone who can skate with me."

If the media circus looked like Game Seven of the finals, my body felt like it was Game Eight. For one thing, the trade had exhausted me. I had come to Los Angeles and done ten straight days of interviews, photo sessions, radio talk shows, "live" insta-cam interviews and Q and A's with what seemed like every media outlet in California and across the country.

Right away I realized I wasn't quite dealing with folks who make hockey their national pastime. When we were shooting a photo session for an L.A. magazine, the stylist started pulling on the right side of my jersey, trying to get it out of my pants. Well, I know I'm not the most famous athlete in the world, but hockey fans who have seen me play know I always leave the right side of my jersey tucked into my pants. It's a superstition and I'm serious about it. So serious that I have it attached in there with Velcro.

"You don't want that in there," she said, ripping at it. "It looks so sloppy." And my first thoughts were, "Uh-oh, we're in for a long, hard road here."

When my agent and good friend Michael Barnett came to Victoria to see me he was shocked. "You look like you look in February," he said. And he was right. I was already down weight, which usually doesn't start until the stretch drive. I was also worrying about my new team. Our coach, Robbie Ftorek, seemed decent and capable. I knew him from the WHA. He was the league's leading scorer the year I signed. But Robbie wasn't skating the team nearly hard enough.

Another problem was our depth. We had the 1987 Rookie of the Year at left wing, Luc Robitaille, a great underrated center, Bernie Nicholls, Dave "Stitch" Taylor and a few other quality players, but we were a team without a lot of talent. We didn't draw a lot of fans either. Of the ten smallest crowds in the league the previous year, six of them involved the you-know-whos. But somehow, in some way I knew even then that we were going to build a great team in Los Angeles and that much as I missed the Oilers, a new chapter of my life had started.

Nearly two years later, as our plane headed home, I decided we weren't doing half bad. The year before, to the astonishment of the entire hockey world, we had knocked my old team, the Stanley Cup champions, out of the playoffs in the first round. Now despite a difficult season, we had the chance to do it again, this time to the Flames, who had burned up the league during the regular season.

And that's exactly what we ended up doing — dumping the Flames — in one of the tightest, most thrilling games I've ever been in. Before our home crowd, we ended Calgary's hopes for a second Cup. Of course, the Oilers then blew us out in four, and went on to win the championship that great team deserves. They have, without question, become the best team in the league, and I know how hard they have worked for their success.

Anyway, for a thousand reasons, I was as happy as I've ever been. And the best thing was, people were saying we'll never win a Stanley Cup in Los Angeles and that I'll never win another MVP.

Just the kind of pressure I love. I've been under it my whole life.

1

Tales of the Blue Goose

I have to admit, my childhood was a little different from most.

I could skate at two. I was nationally known at six. I was signing autographs at ten. I had a national magazine article written about me at eleven and a thirty-minute national television show done on me at fifteen. I turned pro and kept going to high school! Didn't every kid's father flood the backyard in the middle of the winter, put up floodlights, set up nets and have hockey games going from noon to ten at night? Wasn't every kid playing lacrosse, baseball, hockey, street hockey and running cross-country, all at the same time?

I always thought so. Actually, come to think of

it, I never stopped to think about it. I just felt like I was the happiest kid in Canada. Until I was about twelve. That's when I realized I was the *un*happiest.

My hero as a kid was a man with constant headaches, ulcers and ringing in his ears. He's a funny little guy who stays up drinking coffee every night until 3:00 in the morning even though he's got to be at work at 8:00 the next day. He doesn't have to work if he doesn't want to, yet he never misses a day. In fact, he can now afford anything he wants — any house, any car — but he won't take any of it. He stays in his same house driving his same car, teaching kids the same way he always has, believing in the same things he always has.

He was my hockey instructor. He was also my lacrosse, baseball, basketball and cross-country coach, not to mention my trainer and chauffeur. He's still my coach, but he's also my agent, manager, amateur lawyer, business partner and best friend. He doesn't have a college degree, but he's probably the smartest guy I know. He's taught some other good players, too. He has kind of a funny, pointed nose and a crinkly smile and his hair sticks up sometimes. He can't go anywhere in Canada without people saying hello to him.

His name is Walter, but I always call him Wally. Or Dad. I'm crazy about his wife, Phyllis, too. I've sometimes said that everything I have I owe to hockey, but I guess that's not true. Everything I have I owe to them.

"Don't get bigheaded on me," my father would

always say. "No matter how good you are, there's always someone better." And I've always remembered that.

"Follow through whatever you commit to," he was always barking at me, and I try to do that. In my eleven-year pro hockey career, I think I've only missed twenty-six games and one speech.

He tried to teach me values. One day when I was eleven, I played a really bad game. I just wasn't into it, and he took me aside. There was purple smoke coming out of his ears. "You can't play a bad game," he yelled at me. "People are going to judge you on how you perform *every night*. Never forget that." And I tried not to. But about ten years later, during the 1983 Stanley Cup, we'd just lost Game Three and we were down three games to none to the Islanders. We were practicing and afterward my dad came down to me and said, "Why did you practice today?"

"Because we had to," I said. "Everybody had to."

"Well, you shouldn't have. You just wasted your time and theirs. You didn't give an effort."

That was the last we talked about it until later that summer. We were at my grandmother's house and she was out in the sun working in the garden, and my dad comes up to me and says, "Look at that. She's seventy-nine and she's still working hard and you're twenty-three and when you're in the Stanley Cup finals, you won't even practice!"

Ever since then, the highest compliment you can pay me is to say that I work hard every day, practice or game, and that I never dog it. Bobby Orr once said of Mario Lemieux: "On sheer ability,

Mario is good enough to win scoring titles with a broken stick. On pure talent, he's the best there is. But Wayne almost never disappoints you. He comes to work every night." And if it's true, it's thanks to my dad.

Then again, not everything he said was brilliant. He used to play Junior B hockey — he once got a tryout with the Toronto Marlboroughs, Canada's most famous junior franchise, but he got the chicken pox and got cut — and he was pretty good, too. He was a great finesse player, but he just didn't have the size. When I was four and five years old, I was the stick boy for his teams and he'd give me bits of advice. He'd always say, "Son, never skate behind the net." So one night I was watching him warm up and what did he do? He skated behind the net and this guy took a slap shot and, whap, cracked him right in the noggin. Out cold. Then one time he said, "Son, if you go up the middle for a pass, never look back. The guy in front of you will step up and knock you out cold." So one night I'm watching a game, he turned back to see the pass and, crack, the guy laid him out. Not only was he out cold but he lost all his front teeth. Is that what you mean, Dad?

The things he's had to put up with because of me you wouldn't believe. One time, he was in an office fixing a teletype machine. That's his job. The secretary there asked him where he was from and he said, "Brantford." So the lady asked him if he knew Wayne Gretzky and he said, "Yeah." So now the woman proceeds to go off on me, saying how overpaid I was, how overrated I was, how overeverything

I was. Wally just listened and didn't say a word. Then the phone rang, and the lady answered it.

The voice on the other end was from my dad's office. "Is Walter Gretzky there?"

The lady turned purple and ran out of the office. My dad loves to tell that one.

My dad could be egotistical about how well things have turned out for us, but he's not. He's the exact same guy he was when he first taught me to skate. When I come in wearing a nice suit, he'll say, "Uh-oh, how much did you pay for that?"

"About a thousand dollars."

"A thousand dollars? Are you nuts?" And he'll go crazy about how I'm wasting my money and I could get a fine suit for $200 down the street. He'll never change and I love that. When I started making big money, I got him to quit his job so I could take care of him and let him relax. He was in an accident a long time ago that damaged his inner ear, and it rings all the time. He has ulcers and when he's tired, which is all the time considering he can't sleep until 3:00 A.M., he gets awful headaches. So he agreed to try it. He took a six-month leave of absence from his job with Bell Canada. On the last day, he either had to be back at work at 8:00 the next morning or he was done for good. He called me and said, "Wayne, how can I tell my kids not to quit and then quit myself?" The next morning at 8:00, there he was, back on the job. His fellow workers almost dropped their coffee cups.

My parents won't change. Every time I try to buy them something, they refuse it. My dad drove the same old model blue Chevrolet station wagon for years. He called each one of them The Blue Goose. He'd drive them 200,000 miles until the thing was down to four bald tires and a muffler and then he'd buy another one. Every time it would break down, he'd say to me, "Wayne, when I get my shiny new black Cadillac, this won't happen." And so as soon as I started making good money, I brought home a shiny new black Cadillac and parked it in his driveway.

He hardly drove it for two years. "The old Goose is still good," he'd say. "It's only got 180,000 miles on it."

One time I tried to buy them a beautiful mansion in Brantford. Our house was nice, but it was small. They wouldn't accept it. "Too fancy," they decided. So I bought them an empty lot and told them to design their own home and I'd pay for it. They said they'd think about it. I had to go to Europe for a while and when I came back, they'd sold the lot and put an addition on their house. "This is my house," Wally said. "This is where I'm staying." So we bought him a fishing boat and a cottage on a lake near Brantford and just handed him the keys. He hasn't sold that yet.

My dad is the stubborn son of immigrants who started a vegetable farm twenty minutes outside Brantford, Ontario, in 1932. My grandmother, Mary, was born in Poland and emigrated to Canada when she was twenty-six. My grandfather, Tony, came from Russia before World War I in order to enlist. Tony and Mary were full of life. When I was a boy I used to follow my grandfather around while he did his chores. And the first chore was always the same. Seven in the morning he'd go down in the wine cellar and have a little shot of homemade wine out of a big old keg. This stuff would make your ears tingle and then shoot right down to your toes. Then he'd go up to breakfast and my grandmother would smell it on him and scold him.

My grandmother was a tough lady. She loved Frank Mahovlich and all-star wrestling, so you know what I mean. I remember I was playing in a game in Brantford once and a guy named Paul Reinhart was checking me. He had me pinned against the boards, right in front of Grandma. There was no glass there. Next thing I know, Grandma was taking her purse and whapping him over the head as hard as she could, yelling, "You leave my boy alone!" Next to Dave Semenko, I'd have taken Grandma any day.

Tony died in 1973 and that was the hardest day of my life until the day my grandmother herself died. After suffering with leukemia for thirteen years she finally passed away. She was eighty-five. For most of those thirteen years, my mother and sister, Kim, took care of my grandmother and my dad took care of the farm. They worked their butts off to keep my grandmother alive and to keep that farm in the family. That's why there's nothing too good for my parents. Those two people have sacrificed everything for me, my brothers and sister and our family. After my grandmother died, my mom took in our Aunt Ellen and has cared for her ever since. Aunt Ellen isn't easy to take care of. She has Down syndrome. She's about forty-five now and goes to a family living group for the elderly and handicapped that she really loves.

A lot of people know about my dad, but the sacrifices my mom made to put me into the NHL never get talked about. Not going out on Friday nights because I needed a new pair of skates, or holding off on buying new curtains because I needed new hockey sticks, endless hours of driving us to distant arenas, waiting through practices and driving us back, things like that. And yet she never complained.

The funny thing is, my mom isn't even that big a hockey fan. She only wanted the kids to be happy . . . and safe. I remember one time, after I'd signed with Indianapolis, they flew in to see the opener against Bobby Hull and Winnipeg. They were in the hotel and it was about 4:30 in the afternoon before the game when she saw Bobby sitting in the corner with a couple of other players. So she got up, walked over to him and said, "I'm Phyllis Gretzky, and I don't want you hurting Wayne in those corners tonight." To this day, Bobby Hull kids me about that.

And if you think my mom worried about me in the corners, you should have seen her with Glen, my little brother. I'm the oldest, followed by my sister Kim, who is two years younger than me, followed by Keith, five years younger, followed by Glen, seven years younger, and Brent, twelve years younger. Glen was born with club feet. He's had three different operations on them. They even put a pin through his bone, but it made it almost impossible for him to play hockey, his feet hurt so much.

Yet nobody, not even me, practiced as hard as Glen. All the other kids would have gone home when it turned dark and cold but Glen would still be out there, skating around pylons.

It was a hard thing to live with because he wanted to be great as much as I did, but he was held back by his feet. I remember a television crew was in my house interviewing the whole family. They asked my dad why all the other kids started skating at two but Glen waited until he was six. My dad said, "Well, he had a bit of a foot problem." And across the room we could all see poor Glen, head down, tears streaming down his face.

The more determined he was to play the more it would worry my parents to a frazzle. Finally, the pain became too great and he gave it up. He's a real estate agent in Edmonton now, slick and smart. He was always the smartest one in the family. Brent always tells people that Glen was the one who brought the books home all the time. "We'd bring the books home, too," Brent says, "but he *opened* them."

Brent was three when I left home and I didn't really get to know him like I do now. When I'd come home, it was almost like he was more my fan than my little brother. He'd ask me for autographs for friends at school. It's too bad we didn't have more time together because the kid is just great. He pops out of bed at 6:30 every morning and goes twenty-five hours a day with this huge smile on his face. He's a lot like me, cocky. I told him once, "Brent, the next car I win, it's yours."

"Forget that, Wayne," he said. "I'll win my own."

And he refused to let me give him one.

Brent has a real chance to make it in the NHL. For one thing, he can really play. For another thing, he doesn't let all the grief he has to take with the last name Gretzky get him down. He's been pushed out of line in the school cafeteria. "You're just a Gretzky!" the kids would yell. And, like all my brothers, he's had coaches purposely not play him because of me. Brent shrugs it off, no problem.

The expectations, the pressures, the desire to cut him down to size probably fell even more heavily on Keith, since he was the one who had to follow me. He once said there were two things he didn't want. One was to play in Edmonton and the other was to wear 99. I don't blame him. Keith has great talent. At twelve years old, he had 115 goals compared to my 105. If his name was Keith Smith or Keith Jones, he'd be a rising young star in an NHL organization. But as it is, people are all asking him why he's not breaking my records. For that, I feel terrible.

Probably the only one of us who wouldn't like to change their name now and again is Kim. She could have been as successful an athlete as any of us. She was a great runner, tall and fast as the wind. She'd win 100-yard dashes for her age group by ten feet. People said if she kept at it, she had a chance to run in the Olympics. But one day she slipped on an icy curb and cracked her ankle, and it never really healed. Yet she's not the least bit bitter. She works for the Canadian National Institute for the Blind and never thinks about what might have been. She knows how to be happy.

Kim lives in my grandmother's old farmhouse now and, just lately, the strangest things have been happening. It started one morning when she plugged in the teakettle. She took a long shower and came out to find the kettle unplugged and the stove turned on. Another morning, not long after, she walked through the living room and found all the chairs around the dining room table pulled out as if there had been guests. "It was like Grandma had a meeting that night," she said. Then late one night she woke up with a start after her dog jumped on the bed. She heard a sound like a newspaper's pages being turned from somewhere else in the house. She turned on the lights and investigated, but couldn't find a thing, but the dog wouldn't stop whining. My dad says Grandma never did like dogs in the house.

I hope it's my grandmother. She belongs in that house. I'd like her to know that we had a little daughter and that the old place still has a special meaning for me. For one thing, it's probably where I scored my first goal. I beat grandma on the stick side with a little rubber ball and a souvenir hockey stick she'd gotten at a Chicago Blackhawks game. She was my designated goalie. We'd all be sitting out at my grandparents' farm on the Nith River, about twenty minutes outside Brantford, watching "Hockey Night in Canada." We *never* missed "Hockey Night in Canada." She'd pretend her legs were the posts and she'd try to stop me from scoring. The poor lady got a lot of welts on her legs that way.

I learned to skate on that river in the winters. In

the summers, I'd take pucks and slap them against the side of the farmhouse. I remember one time my grandfather had just finished putting in a new window in the house after I'd broken the last one with a slightly off-the-mark shot. He was standing back admiring the beauty of the new one when — SMASH! — I put another puck through it. For a senior citizen, he sure could move.

I had a serious addiction to hockey. I'd drag my dad over to the park every day and make him sit out there freezing his buns until bedtime. He finally got so cold he did something crazy. He turned our backyard into a hockey rink. The Wally Coliseum. The first time he did it I was four. He cut the grass down real short in the fall, waited until the ground froze, covered it with a half-inch of snow, set the sprinkler in the middle and turned it on — all night. The backyard is small, so the rink covered it all. People thought he was crazy, but this way he could watch me from the warmth of his seventy-degree kitchen.

One winter he sent my mom to the hardware store to get a new sprinkler. When she came back she was steaming. "I'll *never* do that again," she said. "People thought I was crazy, buying a lawn sprinkler in February."

When I was thirteen, my friend John Mowat and I decided we were going to help my dad out and make the nets. We worked an entire Saturday in the basement, building the perfect NHL-size goal. When we finally got it done, we were so proud of ourselves — until we realized we couldn't get it out the door. We had to cut the thing in thirds just to get it outside. I guess all that time on the ice had frozen our brains.

All I wanted to do in the winters was be on the ice. I'd get up in the morning, skate from 7:00 to 8:30, go to school, come home at 3:30, stay on the ice until my mom insisted I come in for dinner, eat in my skates, then go back out until 9:00. On Saturdays and Sundays, we'd have huge games, but nighttime became my time. It was sort of an unwritten rule around the neighborhood that I was to be out there by myself or with my dad. I would just handle the puck in and out of these empty detergent bottles my dad set up as pylons. Then I'd set up targets in the net and try to hit them with forehands, backhands, whatever. Then I'd do it all again, except this time with a tennis ball, which is much harder to handle.

I was so addicted that my dad had big kids come over to play against me. And when the kids wanted to go home, I'd beg them to stay longer. I suppose that's how I was always able to do well against bigger guys later on. That's all I could get to play against.

I'll never forget that house on Varadi Avenue. It had three bedrooms, one for my parents, one for my sister and one little eight-by-six room for me and my two brothers. Brent was still a baby and sleeping with my parents. All I wanted from life was the two sticks my dad would get me for $1.99 down at the neighborhood Woolco. They'd last me two months and then he'd go buy two more.

Nowadays, people come up to me, dragging their kids behind them, and say, "Wayne, tell my son to practice three hours a day like you did." And I always say, "I'm not going to tell him to practice three hours a day. Let him go ride his bike if he wants." Nobody told me to practice three hours a day. I practiced all day because I loved it. All my friends would leave the ice and say, "Let's go to the movies," but I never wanted to. The only way a kid is going to practice is if it's total fun for him — and it was for me.

By this time I was driving my parents bananas. My dad was going crazy trying to find a league for me to play in. The problem was, you had to be ten to play in any of the leagues around Brantford. Finally, when I was six, they let me try out in the Brantford Atom league and I made it. I was playing with ten-year-olds and I thought it was the most fun since the invention of ice itself. I wore number 11, played the third line and scored one goal all year. But the best part was the day I got my first hockey jock. Major moment.

Not only was I six, I was a puny six, which meant the sweaters they had for the players looked like ballroom drapes on me. My sweater was so big it was constantly getting caught on my stick on my shooting side. One day my dad tucked the shooting side into my pants and it's been there ever since. Not that I'm superstitious or anything.

At the end of that year, I can remember coming home in my dad's car after the year-end banquet and crying.

"What's wrong?" my dad asked me.

"I didn't win a trophy," I cried. "Everybody won a trophy but me."

And my dad said something to me right then that I'll never forget.

"Wayne, keep practicing and one day you're gonna have so many trophies, we're not gonna have room for them all."

And he was right. Lots of kids as gifted as I was never had somebody like him to keep them on the right line. I don't know where I'd be without him, but I know it wouldn't be in the NHL.

The next year I scored 27 goals for that team, then 104 the next, then 196 the next.

And then came the year that was a dream and a nightmare at the same time. It was the first time unhappiness really crept into my life. I was ten years old, still four feet four, and I scored 378 goals in sixty-nine games. I won the scoring race by 238 goals. People ask me how that happened — it's still far and away the record for that age group — and I don't really know, except that I had a five-year head start on most of those kids. See, kids usually don't start playing hockey until they're six or seven. Ice isn't grass. It's a whole new surface and everybody starts from ground zero. You can be six or thirty-six, if it's your first time on skates, you're going to be wobbly. By the time I was ten, I had eight years on skates instead of four, and a few seasons' worth of ice time against ten-year-olds. So I had a long head start on everyone else.

But those 378 goals were the beginning of the end for me in Brantford. First of all, it created national attention. By the age of ten, I'd done more interviews than some NHL players. That was the year I got the nickname "The Great Gretzky." A writer named John Herbert from the London, Ontario newspaper hung that on me. I didn't really like the name then and it still embarrasses me now. My friends call me Gretz.

Anyway, that 378 started people's minds to warping. There was even a wild rumor that the New York Rangers were going to buy the entire Brantford Pee Wee franchise, just so they'd have first rights to me when I turned pro. *Right.* All that publicity and attention on a ten-year-old was getting hard to handle. Hockey was no longer just fun. It became fun mixed with doses of fame and jealousy and ugliness. I'd go into out-of-town tournaments and they'd have posters up, saying, SEE WAYNE GRETZKY, TEN-YEAR-OLD SCORING ACE, HERE SATURDAY. You've got to understand, when my wife looks at old home movies of me as a kid, she can't believe how quiet I was. "You never said anything!" she says. And it's true. I was incredibly quiet. So you can see how attention like that was a shock for me.

It got so bad that sometimes at tournaments I'd switch team jackets with our goalie, Greg Stefan, just to keep people from bugging me. Greg and I were about the same height and had the same color hair, so we'd switch and he'd wear the jacket that said GRETZKY and I'd wear STEFAN. The problem was, he didn't know how to spell my name, so when people would ask him for my autograph, he'd write it with an "s" instead of a "z." Somewhere there are people who think I'm so dumb I can't spell my own name.

My sudden stardom didn't sit too well with the

parents of the other kids. It was never the kids who were the problem, it was always the (alleged) grown-ups. They'd call me a puck hog. We lost six games all year, had our season's stats go up in the Hockey Hall of Fame, and they were worried about how much I had the puck. People would actually come to the game with stop watches and time how long I held the puck. People would boo me. Once, at a big tournament in my own arena in Brantford, I got booed when I was introduced. That's tough to take when you're ten years old.

To an extent, now I can understand where those parents were coming from. Maybe I was a little showy. I was ten years old and I had my now-famous "kick" when I'd score a goal. I'd kick my knee up high and bring my right arm down like I was pulling down on a train whistle. But I wasn't trying to be cocky. I got it from a guy in my dad's Junior B league where he coached. His name was Dave Pay and he played for St. Catharines. I don't think he ever even made it to pro hockey, but I was a stick boy in that league and I thought everything Dave Pay did was cool, so I started doing it.

I guess parents were just trying to protect their own kids' development in hockey. If I had the puck, that meant their kid didn't. But I went out of my way to give it up. It takes a lot of passing to reach 120 assists in 79 games. I've thought about it now as an adult, and I think if I really had been a selfish player, my teammates wouldn't have liked me. But that just wasn't true. It was always the parents.

One day the goalie had only five shots on goal the whole game and he let in three. We lost 3-2. His father came up to me afterward and called me every name in the book. Parents would sit in the stands and do nothing but scream at me. I never understood why a parent would do that. I mean, did they ever stop and think how that made *their* kid feel?

They were all sure I was going to be exposed as talentless. All along the way, people just couldn't accept what I was doing. They'd see the numbers, the 378s, and just refuse to believe they were real. "It's got to be a fluke," they'd say, and they kept saying it. When I was ten, they were saying I'd be washed up at twelve. When I was twelve, they were saying I'd be washed up by fourteen. When I was fourteen, they said fifteen. It became a good luck charm in our family. As long as people were saying I was doomed, we knew we were in good shape.

Gretzky-bashing was popular in every sport I played as a kid — lacrosse, baseball, hockey, whatever. And it just got relentless. One time an opposing baseball coach came up to me before a game and said, "You won't live to see Christmas, Gretzky." Maybe it would have been amusing to an adult, but to a kid, it was tough to take.

I remember one lacrosse game, I had scored two goals and nine assists. We won 11-2, and I had set this one kid up on six of the goals. We played the next day and we won again and this time it was the reverse — I scored nine goals and two assists. I could've played a baseball game that day, but since it was the lacrosse playoffs, I picked lacrosse. After the game, I was sitting there, having a pop, having fun with my friends on the team, when that same kid's mother came up to me and said, "Wayne, you should have gone to the baseball game today." I went home, locked my door and cried all night.

What I was finding out is that excellence has its price. The trick is to be good at something without making the rest of the world mad at you. But when you're a kid, all you feel is confused. And hurt.

My dad could take it, but my mom couldn't. She stopped sitting with him at hockey games. My dad was famous in the city, but not too many people knew my mom. People would yell rotten things at my dad and my mom would get so upset that she started finding other seats. She still does it today. And she doesn't forget, either. Now, when some two-faced person from those days comes up and wants to be her best friend, she lets them have it. "How can you expect me to talk to you now when you know ten years ago, you were calling my kid every name in the book?" Don't mess with my mom.

I think that part of my life shaped my personality. For one thing, I grew up fast. I had the world's shortest childhood. By the time I was thirteen, I had an agent. I had traveled all over Canada. When I was thirteen, I played in front of a sold-out, 15,000-seat arena. I've been told that Jean Beliveau, the great Montreal Canadien, even came one day to see me play. I had seen adults at their best and their worst. I learned that jealousy is the worst disease in life. And I learned that there are always going to be some people who want to bronze you and some who want to hang you and you can't get too carried away with either kind. Because I was afraid to be thought of as cocky or mouthy, I became even more shy. Enough people disliked me just for the way I played hockey. I didn't want to start talking and give them something else not to like. I didn't want to get hurt any more.

And I decided one more thing. I wanted to get out of that town.

The pressure and the backbiting and the name-calling got so bad that it affected my hockey. I wore a pair of white gloves the year I was fourteen and people started calling me The White Tornado. "What's he need those gloves for?" people would holler at the coach. "He ain't playing at night!" But those gloves just happened to be the best they made. They were light for feel and still warm. To me, it was worth the teasing, but I only wore them that one year.

That year and the next were the two worst of my life. My dad didn't know what to do about it and neither did I. It's like we were stuck.

But when I was fourteen, a phone call came from Heaven. A friend of mine, a man named Sam McMaster, asked if I'd like to come to Toronto, join a team there, and live with the family of one of the players.

"Are you kidding?" I asked. "I'd *love* to."

My parents, unfortunately, were against it.

"You can't," my dad said when I asked him.

"Why?"

"Just because."

"I know what it is. You're afraid I'll fall into the wrong crowd. You're afraid I'll start messing with drugs in the big city, is that it?"

I could tell by his face that it was.

"Well, tell you what," I said. "You give me some money, tell me what drugs you want, and I'll be back in a half hour with it, doesn't matter what it is."

My dad just kind of looked at my mom, sighed and said, "OK."

The funny thing is, I was just bluffing. I had no idea where to get drugs in Brantford.

So at fourteen, I left home. I was supposed to play for the Bantam team in Toronto, but the coaches there thought I was good enough to try Junior B, so I did. I was fourteen years old, playing with the Toronto Young Nationals, trying to avoid being checked by twenty-year-old guys with mortgages. Me, I was 135 pounds. But I got two goals my first game and I knew I'd be all right.

Looking back on it, those years in Toronto were no way for a kid to live. I was awfully lonely, living with somebody else's family, coming home on weekends, trying to feel part of my own family by talking to them on the telephone. But what choice did I have? I didn't leave Brantford to go play better hockey. I left because the people drove me out. In Toronto, I could go to school and nobody but the principal knew who I was. I could play hockey at night and nobody would boo me or bring out their stopwatches. Nobody cared what color my gloves were. In fact, I was terrified people would catch on to me at all. My one good friend at school, Brian Mizzi, happened to show up at a hockey game one night when I got four goals. He cornered me the next day and said, "That was you, wasn't it!?!" I begged him never to tell anybody, and he never did. Being unknown was too nice to mess up.

When I think about it now, there is a lot of sadness in me still. I'd left home for good at fourteen. I missed Dad and Mom and the whole family like crazy, the way we were so close. I never did get to see Brent grow up. To him, for quite a while, I'm afraid I wasn't so much a big brother as a hockey superstar who spent the night now and again.

And you know what the saddest part is? From the time I went to The Soo until this very day, I have only been home for Christmas twice.

2

Life in Skalbania

The last place I wanted to start out my professional hockey career was in Sault Ste. Marie. I told people I didn't want to go to Sault Ste. Marie. My dad wrote a letter to the management of Sault Ste. Marie and told them not to draft me because I would not, under any circumstances, report to Sault Ste. Marie. Naturally, I was drafted by Sault Ste. Marie. It was 1977.

My dad has always said my life has been predestined and that no matter what he or I do to screw it up, we will always land on a soft spot. The Soo is a perfect example. It turned out to be the best thing for my career.

The Soo Greyhounds were run by this great Italian guy who was as crazy about hockey as he was about linguini, Angelo Bumbacco. We flew up to see Angelo to tell him we weren't going to play for him. But as soon as I met him and saw the town, I knew I was going to play there. For one thing, they were going to let me live with a family I liked, the Bodnars. Steve Bodnar used to play in Pee Wee and Novice with me. For another thing, the coach, Muzz MacPherson, told me I was going to be exhausted from all the playing time I got. For a third thing, they wrote into the contract that if I didn't make the team or I was injured before I left, they'd pay the cost of four years at any university in North America. My family loved that.

I was hooked on Mr. Bumbacco, too. That first week, he came up to me and said, "Where's your coat?" I didn't have a decent one. So he took me to a nice clothes store and bought me a beautiful overcoat. I was thrilled that a general manager would care that much. That coat meant the world to me.

The Soo was where I started wearing number 99. I'd always wanted to wear 9, because Gordie Howe wore 9, but Brian Gualazzi was already wearing it. So I wore 19 for awhile and then 14. That was the same year Phil Esposito and Ken Hodge got traded from Boston to the New York Rangers, where Rod Gilbert already had number 7, so Esposito took 77 and Hodge took 88. It was the first time anybody could remember anyone wearing anything past 31. So Muzz told me one day, "Why don't you try 99?"

I figured everybody would laugh at me, and I was right. The first time I wore it, in Niagara Falls, some guy hollered out, "Hey, Gretzky, this isn't football . . . 13, 72, hike!" But I got three goals that night (a field goal), and after that you couldn't have torn that number off me. Not that I'm superstitious.

I was a cocky kid then. At my first practice in The Soo I skated up to Muzz and I asked him how many points the Junior A scoring champ, Mike Kaszycki, had the year before.

"One hundred and seventy," said Muzz.

"No problem," I said. "I'll break that."

Actually, for the first week, I think Muzz was a little worried that he'd wasted a great draft choice — third overall — on such a puny sixteen-year-old. And maybe I was a little nervous, too, because I stunk up those practices. But I got three goals and three assists in my first game and Muzz was my biggest fan in town from then on.

I remember after that first game, they gave me a bottle of Brut as Player of the Game.

"What's this 'Brut' stuff?" I asked my buddy Doug Kimbell afterwards.

"Aftershave lotion," he said.

"What am I supposed to do with aftershave lotion?"

I was making $25 a week, which seemed like serious money back then. I mean, what were my needs? I had enough to stop every day after my high school classes for a piece of apple pie and ice cream at a place right across from the rink. What else was there in life? I never had a girlfriend in high school because I never had time. I was playing Junior A hockey and going to school at the same time. Who had time for girls? I never even went to a prom. All I had time to do was study (great in math, terrible in English) and play. Of course, that wasn't easy. I'd get home from a road trip at 3:00 A.M., get about four hours of sleep and have to be at class at 8:00 A.M. One time we landed at 3:00 A.M. and Muzz was so angry at the way we had played that he made us go straight to the rink and practice in our coats and ties. We won the next night and I sure am glad Muzz wasn't superstitious.

That might have been one reason I never did get my high school degree. I'm one credit short. I got a letter once telling me all I needed to do was send them $35 and they'd send me my diploma. Well, if you can *buy* it for $35, what's the value of it? Look, I know the value of an education. I think guys who pass up the professional leagues out of high school and sign with a college are making the right choice — for them. My life has gone pretty well so far without it, so I think I'll just leave it alone.

The Soo was also the first and last time I used the "I'm Wayne Gretzky" to get something. The tradition on the team was to make the rookies run down Queen Street in nothing but a jock and a hockey sock over our faces. So that's exactly what I was doing when a police car pulled up. All my life, I'd never rebelled, never been in trouble, and now this. About to be busted wearing a jock. So I thought I'd try my luck.

"It's OK, officer," I stammered. "I'm Wayne Gretzky!"

"No, you're not," said the cop. "I know Muzz MacPherson and he doesn't associate with weirdos, so you can't be Wayne Gretzky."

I was stunned. They took me down to the station in a paddy wagon and threw me in a cell. My world was coming apart. I was about to cry. I was trying to think of a way to get out of this when I said, "Hey, I get one call, don't I?" Just then, all the veterans and Muzz came around the corner, along with the cop, laughing their heads off. It was all a set-up and I'd fallen for it hook, line and sinker.

They called me "Pretzel" in The Soo, because I skate kind of hunched over. But something must have been working. I broke that all-time Junior A scoring record that first year. Unfortunately, I broke it the same year as Bobby Smith of Ottawa, only Bobby massacred it — he got 192 points. He went on the next season to become NHL Rookie of the Year for the Minnesota North Stars. Me, I figured I'd stay in The Soo, that is, until Muzz left.

Muzz resigned over personal problems with management, and I was never quite sure what they were. All I knew was he was gone and replaced by Paul Theriault. Theriault immediately set out to change my style. He wanted me to be in exactly the right place all the time, which is exactly the wrong place for me. I go where the puck is going, not where it was. The thing that makes hockey great is the zillions of possibilities in every game. To play it well, you need room to improvise. To make me play in a certain spot in a certain time was like taking one of my skates off. I hated the guy. Without Muzz, The Soo suddenly felt a lot colder.

I wanted to play pro, and thought I might be ready. My agent, a family friend we'd used since I was fifteen, Gus Badali, started making calls. The NHL didn't allow underage juniors, so our only choice was the World Hockey Association. People made fun of the WHA and its fluorescent orange pucks but if the WHA hadn't existed — and it didn't exist for very long — I might have never gotten my foot into pro hockey. I'd have been stuck in The Soo for another three years with a coach I hated and maybe burned out on the game. But like my dad says, destiny.

It didn't look good. After the World Junior Championships in Montreal the late John Bassett of the Birmingham Bulls offered me a one-year contract for $80,000, but Gus's advice was to turn it down, and I listened to him. Gus was banking on a better deal. Gordie Howe's New England Whalers (now Hartford) offered me a $200,000 signing bonus for an eight-year contract, but backed out at the last minute because they thought they had a chance to make the NHL and were worried about my being underage.

Luckily, the entrepreneur Nelson Skalbania took a chance on me. Skalbania flew me and my parents and Gus up to his house in Vancouver to get to know us. He met us at the airport in a Rolls Royce. It was the first one any of us had ever been in. So what happens? The Rolls smokes all the way to his house. When we pulled up into his driveway, Mr. Skalbania jumped out, disgusted. There was another Rolls in his driveway and it wasn't working, either. So he said to my dad, "Walter, don't ever buy a Rolls."

"Don't worry, Mr. Skalbania," my dad said without cracking a smile. "I never will." To this day, my dad has kept that promise. No problem.

The way Nelson Skalbania interviews people is he runs with them until they're ready to drop. I guess if you don't collapse in front of him, you're hired. His theory was that hockey players weren't in shape. What he didn't know was that I love to run. He and I took off running and talking. We ran about seven miles, and the end of it was straight uphill. I decided to sprint it and wait for him at the top. I was trying very hard not to show that my lungs were about to collapse.

He seemed impressed. I went back to my room and collapsed like a wounded deer. "Oh, God, I'm dying!"

"Shuddup, willya?" my dad whispered. "He'll think you're not in shape."

Finally, I propped myself up long enough to get into his office, followed by my parents and Gus. The first thing he did was look at Gus and say, "How much money do you want?"

We settled for a $250,000 signing bonus, plus $100,000 in the first year, $150,000 in the next two years and $175,000 in the fourth. It was a personal-services contract with Skalbania. If he sold his team, I'd still be working for him.

Years later, Skalbania's choice of this arrangement would be one of the reasons Peter Pockling-ton sold my contract to the Kings. When Peter wanted to raise money by selling shares in the Oil-ers to the public, he realized that it wouldn't look right for him to sell shares in the team but keep my contract to himself. And various laws prevented him from simply transferring my contract to the team.

So there I was, just barely seventeen and I'd already signed a large professional hockey contract. I had worked the whole summer before, pouring gravel in potholes on roads, making $5.00 an hour. It was a big moment for me and for my parents and for Gus. Hockey had been a lot of things before: fun, work, thrilling, troubling, but it had never been well-paying.

Just before Skalbania signed the deal, he looked up from his paper and said, "Are you *sure* you can play?"

"Yessir," I said. "I can play."

The only question was, where?

Skalbania couldn't decide whether I should play for Indianapolis, the team he owned in the WHA, or Houston, the team he was thinking about buying. We got on his private plane to Edmonton — he owed somebody there a favor so that's where we were going to hold the press conference — and he still hadn't decided. Meanwhile, while we were in the air, he had me personally handwrite the contract. I remember I used some of my lined homework paper underneath the sheet he gave me to keep my letters straight. Was I ready for the bigtime or what?

Skalbania picked up the phone in the plane and called the Houston coach.

"Can Gretzky play pro hockey?" he asked the guy.

"Well, I'm not sure about his skating," the guy said. "I hear he's not that good of a skater."

"OK," said Skalbania. "Thanks."

And so Skalbania didn't buy the club, we landed the plane in Indianapolis and that's how I became an Indianapolis Racer.

Later on in my life, following the trade to the Kings, writers got to talking about how the NHL would be pushing for wider U.S. acceptance of hockey now that I'd "finally" come to an American team. People must have forgotten my glorious career with the Racers. Actually, I don't blame them. I'd like to forget about it myself.

I, personally, might have killed pro hockey in Indianapolis. In the eight games I played there, I had only three goals and three assists. We drew eleven thousand people for the opener, then six thousand or fewer from then on. I guess maybe they weren't all that excited about this hot new kid from The Soo.

I had a feeling it wasn't going to work there, anyway. They had me signing autographs and selling season tickets in the local mall, and in two hours I'd sign maybe four autographs and sell zero tickets.

Skalbania called me not long after and said, "Wayne, this isn't working. I'm losing $40,000 a game. We've got to move you." He told me he could move me to either Winnipeg or Edmonton and he was going to consider my preference. The bad thing was, he was including two veterans, Peter Driscoll, a fifty-goal scorer, and Eddie Mio, our great young goaltender, in the deal. Here I was, a punk eighteen-year-old, influencing where these grown men were going to play out their careers. At least he told me I was.

Personally, I didn't know anything about Edmonton or Winnipeg. I called Gus and he said, "Pick Edmonton." He said it was an oil town that was booming. Also, it had led the WHA in attendance the year before. If the NHL was going to take a WHA team, they'd want a team with a big arena and a great following. I picked Edmonton.

You should have seen Peter's and Eddie's faces when Whitey Stapleton, our coach, told them to be on a plane in two hours.

Whitey: "You've been traded."

Eddie: "Traded? Where to?"

Whitey: "I have no idea."

Skalbania put us on another one of his famous bound-for-nowhere planes. We didn't know if we were headed for Winnipeg or Edmonton. I'd have hated to be one of his pilots.

Come to think of it, his passengers didn't have it so good, either. When we got in the air, the pilot turned around and said to us, "Boys, who's paying for this flight?"

Neither Peter nor I had any credit cards, but Eddie did. He sort of reluctantly handed over his. The flight cost $4000. Eddie's card had a $600 limit, but the bill got paid.

Finally, the word came: We would play in Edmonton. I found out later that Skalbania had offered to play Winnipeg owner Michael Gobuty in a game of backgammon. If Gobuty won, he'd get me. If he lost, he'd have to give Skalbania a big piece of the Jets. Gobuty finally backed off, which was probably a mistake. Mr. Skalbania is a lousy backgammon player.

I landed in Edmonton with my hockey stuff, the clothes I was wearing, an extra pair of pants and a toothbrush. Welcome to the big time. When we got out of the plane, there was nobody there, no press, no Oiler people, zip. Turns out we landed at the wrong airport. Back in the plane. When we finally got to the right airport and the right press conference, you could hardly understand our answers. We were so hungry we stuffed ourselves with the appetizers they had sitting out for the press.

The next morning, the head coach, Glen Sather, called me into his office and told me I could live with him until I got settled. I thought that was very nice and I accepted. I stayed about three weeks. He also told me another thing that made my eyes bug out.

"One day, we're gonna be in the NHL and one day you're going to be captain of this hockey team," he said. "Remember I told you that."

This was a little hard to believe, considering I was seventeen and the next youngest guy was Dave Hunter and he was twenty. Most of the guys were much older. Right away, the owner, Peter Pocklington, ran us all through this three-day seminar about raising children and family finances. At the end of it, I thought to myself, "Great. As soon as I'm old enough to vote, I'll start worrying about raising children and family finances."

The weird thing is, Pocklington signed me without ever having seen me play. And when I turned eighteen that January 1979 — that very day — he brought a huge cake out to center ice, shaped in the number 99, and had a contract there for me to sign. He was going to pay me $3 million over the next ten years, with options to keep me until 1999. Get it?

That whole week leading up to it, I couldn't decide whether to sign or not. 1999? That was twenty years away! Gus recommended I sign it in case I ever got hurt. That was hard to argue with. I asked my roommate, Ace Bailey, what to do.

"If you're not sure, don't sign it," he said.

"But I've got to," I said. "They're having a cere-mony tonight and everything."

"So sign 'Bob Smith.' "

When I got out there, with Peter and my family and all the TV cameras watching, I actually started to make the B for Bob but then I chickened out and I changed it. That's the weirdest W you ever saw. I never did find out what was in that cake. They took it into the dressing room and one of the guys sat on it. This was a very sentimental team.

Ace taught me a lot of things. He was thirty-three years old with a wife and a son, Todd, but he took me under his wing and we became best friends. The first thing he taught me was to get an extra set of car keys. That way you could come to the game and lock your car doors with the engine running. That's how cold it gets in Edmonton.

I'll never forget the afternoon Ace and I were on the road and overslept our wake-up call by about an hour and a half.

"Gretz!" he hollered. "GRETZ! It's 20 till 7!" Game time was 7:30.

I was a rookie, so naturally I was in a real panic.

"You go!" he said. "They won't miss me."

So he frantically helped me get dressed and out the door and into a cab. I got to the rink about one minute before we went on the ice for our pregame skate-around. I was fine, but there was still no sign of Ace. We were out there for forty-five minutes and still no Ace. When we came in, there was Ace, sitting in his equipment, all sweaty, looking like the rest of us.

"Ace, I didn't see you on the ice," I said. "Where were you?"

He called me over to whisper in my ear. "I didn't get here until five minutes ago," he said. "So I put my equipment on, went into the shower, and got all wet. They never even missed me!"

Ace had an answer for everything. One time, playing Winnipeg I think, I had this pesky guy holding me all night. I couldn't get rid of the guy. Finally, Ace came up and said to me, "I'll get him for you. Get him to chase you and bring him by the bench."

Great, so I got the puck, brought this guy by the bench and next thing I knew, the whistle blew. I looked back and this guy was out colder than a popsicle. Ace had stood up on the bench and knocked him out cold with his stick. When everybody turned to see who did it, Ace was pointing up into the crowd and hollering, "Somebody do something! Somebody threw something from the crowd! Eject that guy!"

Ace. What a beauty. One time Ace had rented a house through the Oiler organization but hadn't yet seen it. He was having a few beers with the boys the night he was supposed to move in and so when he finally went to take a look at it, his vision was a little clouded. He tried to fit the key in and it didn't work. Pretty soon, Ace was trying to spring the garage door by bouncing up and down on it and Cowboy Flett was up on the roof trying to get in through a skylight. That's about when the cops showed up. Turns out they had the wrong house. That house belonged to an old retired couple who were found huddling in the middle of the living room together.

One Christmas Ace's wife told him to go out and get them a Christmas tree. Well, Ace looked and looked but never found one he wanted — until he got back home. There it was, the perfect Christmas tree, right in his own backyard. We cut it down, brought it inside and his wife never knew the difference. But he told me later. He called me over a week after Christmas to try and help him nail it back in place.

Ace wasn't the only thing I liked about the WHA. I knew right away I could play there. It was faster, which I liked, and it was much cleaner than junior hockey, which I *loved*. I was only 155 pounds. One cheap shot and I could have been on my way back to Brantford.

I guess the biggest game I played that year was against the Cincinnati Stingers. My defensive screwup led to a Stingers goal that got us behind 2–1 and Sather immediately benched me. I hadn't been benched since I was six years old! I was fuming, at him and at myself. He finally put me back in the third period and I got a hat trick and we won

5–2. Sather told me later that he thought that game turned my career around. "You could've pouted," he said, "but instead, you came back." Personally, I thought my career was going to be fine. What made me score the three goals was trying to make Sather look like an idiot. Either way, I guess he proved his point.

That was the first time Slats had put any pressure on me at all. He had treated me really well up to then. Both he and his wife, Anne, went out of their way to make me comfortable. Anne had even cooked meals for me when I first got to Edmonton and was staying with them. She's a very classy lady and our relationship remained a very nice one throughout all my years in Edmonton. I liked Glen, too. He was always pretty cool, pretty casual. The bigger the game, the more he acted like it was nothing. He'd either be back in the back room polishing his shoes or maybe hemming the cuffs on his pants. The guy was far and away the best tailor in the WHA. He was always saying, "Hey, you got a little tear in that sleeve. Come into my office and we'll fix you right up."

He was a man who never seemed to sweat. Our locker room could get really hot and yet you'd never see him perspire a drop. Even later, when we'd go to Boston, where the locker room is like a sauna, he'd be sitting there, tie tied and coat buttoned, drinking that styrofoam cup of coffee that never left his hand. In fact, the only time he'd get hot was if somebody cut his shoes with their skate. Then he'd go crazy. "Hey, those were brand new!"

In those days, Slats made it fun. We had this tradition for every game. First, Slats would announce the starting lineup on the other team. We'd all gather around him and after each name we'd holler, "Boo!" or "He sucks!" or "Brutal!" And then he'd announce the names in our starting lineup and it was always "Yeah!" or "Sweet!" or "Oh, he's the best!" It's silly, but hey, whatever works.

But pretty soon I learned that underneath the slick exterior and the fun façade was a guy who couldn't stand to lose. Slats never forgot a loss. His theory was, if you lost but had played well, it was every bit as bad as playing awful and losing. Slats wanted to win so badly that if we lost on the road, he'd change hotels. We must've stayed in every hotel in Boston over the years, because we hardly ever won there.

He was so competitive that he'd chirp at the other team across the glass or on the ice. For instance, he'd yell at Marcel Dionne, "You're out of shape, Dionne," and then Dionne would get so ticked off he'd nearly beat us by himself.

Slats was notorious for yelling at the fans on the road, too. I swear, I can't remember a game when there wasn't some kind of altercation between the fans and Sather. Slats would always stand up behind the bench and the fans back there would scream at him to sit down. "Go (bleep) yourself!" Slats would scream back, and the next thing you knew they were trying to climb the glass to get to him.

We won a lot that year in the WHA. In fact, we made it all the way to the WHA finals. Big deal, there were only six teams. Still, we played Winnipeg for the Avco Cup. That was also the week we got to find out what Pocklington could be like. Peter announced that he was giving each of us a one-person round-trip ticket to any Club Med resort in the world for making the finals. Just before Game Six, down three games to two, he came walking into the locker room with a box. We figured, yes, here's the ticket.

Wrong. He started going around the locker room handing out these skimpy, ugly swimming suits and bottles of Coppertone. We were all sort of blank-faced. I guess that was his idea of an inspiration to win the game, a reminder of the Club Med vacation. When he left, we all laughed so hard our guts hurt. We were so dumbfounded by this man that we went out and played the worst game of the year. Winnipeg scored on their first four shots and we were out of it. Which was good, because I didn't want to see Ace in one of those swimming suits. Naturally, we never got the tickets.

We weren't looking for Peter's perks anyway. All we knew then was that we were playing hockey and we were getting paid for it. Who could ask for more? We had a helluva lot of fun. I got forty-three goals and 104 points and won Rookie of the Year. And naturally, my favorite battle cry was heard all over the league: "Fluke!" One guy wrote, "Sure, he can play junior varsity hockey, but what will happen when he gets to the NHL?"

He wouldn't have to wait long to find out.

3

Miracle in Montreal

Gus was right. The NHL wanted Edmonton and they swallowed us into the league the very next season, 1979–80, along with Quebec, Winnipeg and Hartford. Goodbye, orange pucks. Hello, NHL.

The only lousy thing was that for the fifth straight season, I was going to be a rookie — Junior B, Junior A, OHA, WHA and the NHL. Do you realize how many rookie hazings that is? Too many. I'd had my eyebrows shaved (my landlady had to paint them in for four weeks), woken up on planes to find shaving cream in my hair (the tradition is, nobody says anything to you so you get as many weird stares as possible walking to baggage claim), had my shoes stolen on flights (I walked through the entire Montreal airport once shoeless), and so on. Very adult stuff.

I had been lucky, though. I'd always managed to avoid the ultimate hazing: The Shave.

The Shave involves being tied down and having your, uh, your I-can't-mention-it-in-a-G-rated-book shaved. Actually, you didn't even have to be a player to have this done to you. One time, Ace and Cowboy Bill Flett even managed to nail a sportswriter.

It was the late, great Paul Rimstead of the *Toronto Sun,* and Ace and Cowboy convinced him they needed his help with a bet. Cowboy said he was betting Ace he could lift three people, or about six hundred pounds, on one blanket, all by himself. Soon bets were being laid down everywhere. Ace said, "Rimmer, we need three people on this blanket. Get on." So they put Rimstead, Peter Driscoll and winger Dave Semenko on the blanket, all weighed and stripped. As they started tying all their hands, Rimstead looked up, puzzled.

"Why are you doing that?" he asked.

"So the weight doesn't shift," said Ace.

Once the Rimmer's hands were tied, Semenko and Peter jumped off and Rimmer suddenly realized he'd been had. Shave time.

That was the end of it until the next night. About thirty minutes before game time we suddenly heard this giant motor revving outside the door. In stomped Rimmer, looking like Freddy Kruger, with a chainsaw going full boil. He marched over to our sticks and cut them all in half — about sixty of them. It became known as The Edmonton Chain Saw Massacre.

The young guys all decided we wanted to keep about forty miles away from any of that stuff. We knew that if the team was going anywhere, everybody had to be equal and you're not equal if you're constantly worried about getting the shave. Besides, it looked like we *were* going somewhere. We got our best defenseman, Kevin Lowe, in the first round of the 1979 draft and our great center, Mark Messier, in the third. The irony is, Skalbania had used the money he made from selling me to buy Messier from Cincinnati. Small world. But Mess had a lousy year in Indianapolis — at least he lasted a year — and that's how we got him. Every year, Edmonton fans should send gifts to the city of Indianapolis for their contributions to Oilers hockey.

Kevin and Mess became my two best friends in the world. Kevin and I even got an apartment together. Kevin was a great cook. He could make fondue, roasts, lasagna, even cheesecake.

The first time I saw Mess skate I thought, "My God, how did they get this guy with the forty-eighth pick?" "Moose" as everybody called him then, is just a totally free spirit.

He is also the ultimate competitor. One time, Jamie Macoun of Calgary cheapshotted him. Mess didn't forget. He waited until the next period, at his first chance, and steamrolled him, just flattened him like a pancake. And before Macoun was even down on the ice, Mess was on him. Mess broke his jaw and that put Macoun out for a month. That's the kind of competitor Mess was. He was Slats's kind of guy, Slats's favorite player, with Slats's kind of fire but a hundred times the talent Slats had as a player.

Mess is this monster on the ice, but off it, he's a softie. He's the most generous guy I know. He'd not only give you the shirt off his back, but his shoes, his car and his house. Mess's dad played pro hockey with the Portland Buck-aroos and Mess was the stick boy for a while. I can just see this little 7-year-old yelling, "C'mon, guys, let's get it done!"

On the ice, all he wants to do is win. To me, he epitomizes the difference between hockey players and baseball players. Hockey players want to win championships. Baseball players dream about the Hall of Fame. Forget the Hall of Fame. Give Mess the Stanley Cup.

We knew we were going to lose a ton of games that year, but at the same time there was this feeling that maybe we had a lump of coal here on its way to becoming a diamond. We were oozing talent. My line was B.J. Mac-Donald and Brett Callighen. We had Dave Hunter, the world's greatest checker. We had Semenko, the world's best fighter and a pretty fair stick on the wing. We had your basic crafty veterans: Ace and Cowboy, Dave Dryden (Ken's older brother and a former WHA MVP), Paul Popiel, Ron Low, Lee Fogolin, guys who knew what winning took and were trying to teach it to us. My old friend from Indy, Eddie Mio, was the goalie. In the Edmonton pressure cooker, lifelong friendships were created. We didn't just work together at the job. We lived the job together. And we loved it. Eddie and I became great friends. He was the best man at my wedding.

So here were our NHL dreams, all laid out in an eighty-game schedule. I remember the night before our first game in Chicago, Mess and I were sitting in our hotel room, just sort of staring at each other, going, "Hey, we're in the NHL!" I was eighteen and so was he. Kevin was much older. He was nineteen.

We were all anxious about playing in the BIG league, but, luckily, I was comforted to hear the same old junk about me I'd always heard. One program I picked up said, "Gretzky may have finished third in scoring in the WHA, but, of course, there's no way he'll do it in the NHL." I remember throwing the thing across the locker room. I made up my mind right then and there to finish at least third that year. I knew I wasn't Jesus or God — that's what I called Marcel Dionne of the Los Angeles Kings and Guy (the Flower) Lafleur of Montreal — but I figured I was as good as everybody else. At least, that's what I kept *telling* myself.

We lost our first game, and my first goal didn't come until our fifth game against Glen Hanlon of Vancouver. I went to shoot it and it rolled off my stick and dribbled through his legs. Not a real glorious start to my NHL career, but hey, in the stat books it looks like an end-to-end rush, right?

That year was torture. I had tonsillitis the whole way. I ran a fever, my throat killed me, I couldn't speak. One night in St. Louis it got so bad I had to be hospitalized. I suppose I should have had my tonsils taken out, but I didn't want to miss a game.

So I lived on throat lozenges, aspirin and penicillin.

We had our moments. One day we beat the Montreal Canadiens, 9–1. By the All-Star break, I was going pretty good. I got seven points one night and Al Hamilton barely missed on a goal that would have given me eight and tied the record. I was named second-team for the All-Star game, which thrilled me. I felt like bringing a camera to the game. For all I knew, I'd never be back.

By the fiftieth game, I had twenty-eight goals and fifty assists. With eighteen games left, I was within twenty points of Dionne and Lafleur, who were tied for the lead.

"Dad, I know this sounds crazy, but I think I can catch them," I said.

"You're right," he said. "You're crazy."

But I wasn't. By April 2, at age nineteen years two months, I had my fiftieth goal, the youngest player in the history of the league to get fifty. With three games left, I went to Toronto and got two goals and four assists to tie Marcel at 133. The killer thing was I had an easy shot in the last few seconds. I'd beaten everybody, deked the goalie, an absolute no-brainer. Bo could've flipped it in. Instead, I airmailed it high over the glass. My dad always told me, "Put the puck upstairs," but that was into the attic. Turns out that goal would have given me the scoring title.

It all came down to the last game of the night. I'd finished my season — we'd clinched the last playoff spot by winning or tying nine of our last ten games — and we all went out to celebrate. Marcel was playing in L.A., so it was going to be late before we found out what he had done. Finally I couldn't stand it anymore. I jumped up from the table and called out there. Marcel had gotten enough points to tie me.

I was a bit depressed, but I tried not to show it. Then it was announced that they don't split the Art Ross Trophy for the scoring leader and had given the whole thing to Marcel based on more goals. I didn't know that was the rule until then, and I didn't agree with it, either. What did that say to all the kids who'd heard a thousand times, "An assist is as important as a goal"?

Marcel was cool about it. He said he'd polish the trophy up because he knew I'd be winning it a lot from then on. Marcel could be generous that way. He'd do anything to help the league, but he also knows how to carry a grudge. He's been retired for years, yet he still hates the Kings for dealing him to the Rangers at the end of his career. He refuses to let the Kings have a Marcel Dionne Night for him because he thinks it'll just help them sell tickets.

Even though I've won the Art Ross Trophy nine times, I still believe the rule should be changed, so team play can be honored. To me, the best players in hockey are the ones who make their teammates look good, the ones who make their teams win. Truth is, we were all great goal scorers as juniors. In my book, learning to think "them" instead of "me" is what makes you a professional, and it's what makes you a winner. If there's one thing I'd like to be remembered for, it's that I tried to think of "them" more than "me."

The simple answer is to create the Gordie Howe

Award for the guy who scores the most goals in the season. Give the Art Ross Trophy to the scoring title leader. If there's a tie, both names go on it.

That year they also announced I couldn't win the Calder Trophy as Rookie of the Year. They said my season in the WHA counted as a year in pro hockey, even though my WHA points could not count toward my career totals. It shows you how much the NHL was worrying about the WHA at that time.

I did win the Lady Byng Trophy as the most "gentlemanly" player. Some guys might rather win a case of lipstick, but I was proud of it. The Lady Byng has already had some great names on it — Marcel Dionne, Gil Perreault, Stan Mikita, Bobby Hull. You can say what you want about it, but it meant a lot to me because I know it meant a lot to my parents. I think it proved that they did a good job teaching their kids sportsmanship.

Then, totally out of the blue, I got the call that I'd won the Hart Trophy as the Most Valuable Player. Everybody was shocked, stunned and amazed, but nobody more than me. I couldn't believe it. I think I'm still the only "rookie" to win it, even if only Wally and I recognize it. It's still one of the things I'm most proud of, winning it in my first NHL year. And it made me forget all the other things I'd said that year in regard to hardware.

Of course, some critics weren't about to let me get away clean. "Sure, he's a big scorer," one guy wrote, "but he wouldn't score as many if he were playing for a winning team." That's when Sather jumped to my defense. "Not true," he said. "When you're on a losing club, there aren't as many guys helping you, either. Gretzky doesn't have Bobby Orr passing him the puck, the way Phil Esposito did." I always appreciated that.

Besides, I had a feeling this wasn't going to be a losing team for long. History might show that at the end of that regular season we went into the 1980 playoffs and got swept by the Philadelphia Flyers. But the Flyers were the number one team in the league and we gave them all they wanted. We were close the first two and lost the third in overtime. Bobby Clarke, a killer on the ice, gave us fits, but afterward he said, "The Oilers are going to be heard from for a long, long time."

Personally, I thought we were going to be heard from the very next year. We had maybe the best draft in the history of the league. We got Paul Coffey with our first-round pick, then one of the best right-wingers in hockey history, Jari Kurri, a Finn, in the second; Glenn Anderson, the human scoring machine, in the third; and goaltender Andy Moog in the seventh. Where was everybody else on draft day?

We started 1980–81 absolutely red-hot. They put Semenko on my line and he went crazy. In one stretch he got six goals in seven games. Semenko, of course, acted like it happened all the time. One night, when he had two goals, the other team pulled its goalie. He turned around on the bench and told Sather, "Don't put me in, Coach. If I get another goal, that'll be a hat trick and they'll want another one tomorrow night."

By the halfway point of the season, I was tied

with Dionne again for the scoring lead. Once again, they gave him the halfway-point $500 prize money on the basis of more goals. But I didn't care by then and I still don't. Assists are my game. I'm a play-maker. I get exactly the same size butterflies flying around in my stomach after an assist as after a goal. That year I broke Bobby Orr's single-season assist record of 102 and Phil Esposito's single-season points total of 152 in the same week. I was hot all through the last half of that season. I got thirty-four goals in my last forty games, including five goals and two assists against Mike Liut and St. Louis. And when I tied Esposito's 152 points, it was at 1:52 of the period and it was exactly 1:52 P.M. back in Edmonton. My father and I liked that little bit of coincidence.

Still, teams kept right on defensing me like any minute I'd be exposed for the fluke they were sure I was. Nobody shadowed me. Nobody doubled me. Those were the good old days.

That was the year the U.S. won the Olympic hockey gold medal in Lake Placid, which I thought was the greatest thing to happen to hockey in twenty years. People wonder how the Americans beat the Soviets in 1980, but looking back on it, I don't. The Americans played heroically, the star Soviet players didn't come up big and the Soviets made the mistake of taking maybe the best goaltender in hockey history, Vladislav Tretiak, off the ice in the first period.

I felt sorry for Tretiak then. He's a great friend of mine, a big, warm and funny man. Every time he came to the U.S. he'd say the same thing to me.

"Wayne, get me job as American fullback."

Every time he came, he'd make me drag him to some football game. He was fascinated with NFL fullbacks and he always thought he had the size and talent. Size, yes. Talent, I'm not so sure. Maybe he could've played defense on goal-line stands.

Besides, what more could he want than being the greatest athlete in Soviet history? When my dad, my family and Charlie Henry, a family friend, and I went over there to film a documentary, I couldn't believe how famous this guy was. I don't think we passed a single Soviet who didn't recognize him. And yet when we went to the home of this famous man, this great hero, his apartment was the size of an average hotel suite. It was beautifully decorated, but it wasn't big.

He was proud of his home. He had his gold medals on his display case and all sorts of crystal around. In the Soviet Union, the more famous you are the more crystal you have. He had a little car, but he drove the thing like he was Mario Andretti. Honestly, I'd get in that car with him and just pray we didn't all die. If the speed limit was, say, thirty-five on a street, Vlad would go seventy. And on every corner, the Soviet Army police would just wave at him. Heroes have their privileges there.

Anyway, I was happy for everybody on the American team. But one guy, the goalie, Jim Craig, was riding the high of winning the gold medal when he came into the league with the Atlanta Flames the next year and I remember once when he started chirping, "Hey, Gretzky! Just who the (bleep) do you think you are, anyway?"

I didn't say a word, my stick did the talking. I think I got two goals and two assists in the next thirty minutes, including the game-winner. As the year progressed, I think Jim Craig learned that actions speak louder than words in the NHL.

We finished fourteenth in the league for that season. It was spring 1981, and we celebrated by going to a Billy Joel concert. For one song, he even put on one of my jerseys. In the middle of the concert, somebody came up to us and said, "Guess who you guys get in the playoffs? Montreal!"

Montreal. The Forum. Winners of four straight Stanley Cups in the late seventies. That concert suddenly didn't seem so interesting.

I can still remember sitting in the visitors' locker room before the first game in the Montreal Forum, the cathedral of hockey. I remember it had old blue carpeting and ancient wooden benches. There was an old training table in the middle of the room, and I thought of how many great players had lain there in pain and defeat after games here. Maybe the only thing older than all that stuff in there was Doc, the clubhouse man. He always wore a shirt or a jersey or a hat from the team that had been in before, as a subtle reminder that you were supposed to leave him a little something.

And as we sat in the Forum locker room, we were in awe because even though we were tucked away through a long tunnel and two or three sets of doors, we could still hear that roar of the fans. It was spine-tingling. We felt like the Christians about to fight the lions. The rest of the league thought of us as the WHA holdovers from out west, the kickarounds. The Canadiens were 23–6 in post-season play in their last twenty-nine home games. Lafleur was healthy and ready. Their goalie, Richard Sevigny, predicted that Lafleur would put me "in his back pocket." On top of all that, Sather decided to start Moog, who nobody had ever heard of and who had gone 14–13 in Wichita the year before.

But there was this feeling we all had about that series. For one thing, Slats played the psychological game to perfection against Montreal in that series. The whole week he said things like, "This is going to be the biggest mismatch in hockey history," and "we've got no chance, but we'll be a better organization for it." That took all the pressure off us. To us, it was a win-win situation. If we won, we won. If we lost, we won because of what we'd gained in experience.

For another thing, our guys always got jacked up to play in Montreal, especially Kevin Lowe. Kevin was a great player always, but he seemed to pick it up one more notch when we'd go into the Forum. It meant a lot to him to play well in front of people he knew. The whole team seemed to play well in Montreal. In fact, we used to play so well in Montreal that it became a problem because we'd always stink it up the next night in Quebec City. Sather eventually noticed it, too, and got the schedule changed so that we'd play Quebec first, building up to Montreal. Shows you what kind of power Slats developed. Those schedules aren't supposed to be adjustable at a coach's whim, but Slats could do it.

Anyway, against all odds, we went in there and

swept the Canadiens. Some people called it the biggest upset in Stanley Cup history, and it might have been. In the first game, I got five assists, a playoff record. We beat them 6–3 and after the sixth goal, I skated by their net and patted in the general vicinity of my back pocket for Mr. Sevigny.

We played the second game in Montreal and Andy Moog stood on his head and stopped Lafleur cold on three great saves. They were just absolute dial-911-I've-just-been-robbed jobs. We whipped them again 3–1 and even the Montreal fans applauded. We'd swept Montreal *in* Montreal. Incredible.

We went home to Edmonton and finished them off, 6–2. I got three goals and an assist and Moog played out of his mind. And that's when we realized that the prize for winning that great, historic series was a playoff with the defending Stanley Cup champions, the New York Islanders.

Were we scared? Petrified. Were we going to show it? No chance. That was the series where we even sang on the bench. The entire team kept chanting, "Here We Go, Oy-Lers, Here We Go!" Sure, it was high-schoolish, but we were all barely out of high school. Six of us could still have been playing junior hockey! We didn't know yet how to be cool, unflappable, unemotional professionals. We were still nervous, thrilled, jacked up. Singing just felt right. And every time we'd get in trouble, we'd sing.

We did a lot of singing. We lost four games to two. I personally carried home plenty of souvenir bruises. Dave Langevin and Trottier hit me with some shots that were so hard I thought my kids were going to be born dizzy. Still, we weren't embarrassed. We figured 4–2 wasn't too bad against the dominating team in the league.

Denis Potvin was fantastic. He was their best player. Everybody talks about Mike Bossy, but Potvin was the core of that team. I always respected Bossy for his shot, but I wouldn't be too excited to share a cab with him. I don't know why, but we never got along. Maybe because when he was having his greatest years, I was having mine and he resented it. Or maybe it's just that we're so competitive, we can hardly stand to be in the same room. Maybe if I knew him outside of hockey, I'd like him, but I don't know: in his book, he picked himself on his all-time NHL team, which I think is a monument to self-importance.

Still, we'd beheaded Montreal and taken the champs to six games and gained ten years experience in two weeks. It was an unforgettable season. It was the thrill of my life. Everything I'd ever wanted was coming true. I was playing big-time NHL hockey with a team that was improving all the time, and I was proving I could stay with anybody. The Soo seemed a million miles away. And then I won my second straight Hart Trophy, barely beating Mike Liut by five votes. And, when I finally was able to beat Dionne 164–135 for the Ross trophy, he shook his head. "Gretzky makes me feel like an old man," he said.

Marcel was twenty-nine.

4

The Weak-Kneed Wimp Years

Me, I aged about ten years about six months later during Canada Cup '81. That was far and away the worst experience I've ever had in hockey, from the way it was set up, to the coaching, to the atmosphere, to the way I played, which stunk.

That Cup was run like some kind of boot camp. For six weeks, they skated us two hours in the morning and two in the afternoon, then thirty-five minutes of running or biking on top of all that. By the time we got near the end everybody was whipped. You can't power-train for six weeks. In later Cups, they got it down to an hour and a half practice once a day and that was it.

Then we had too many chiefs and not enough

Indians. We had four coaches and four general managers. We had eight powerful guys, none of them with any power. We had Scotty Bowman as a coach and that would have been fine, if he'd been making the decisions. But we also had Red Berenson, Pierre Page, and Cliff Fletcher, plus another four general managers. I remember we beat the Americans 4–1 in the semifinals. But when we got back to the dressing room, it was more like we'd lost 14–1. Our coaches were screaming at us. Alan Eagleson's people — Alan was the organizer of the Canada Cup — were screaming at us. They all said we were going to get killed if we played like that against the Soviets.

Then they did something I thought was totally wrong and, in fact, sort of pointed out the problem. The night before we played the Soviets for the Cup, they had us all meet in a room at the hotel. We met there at 7:30, but we didn't know why. Nobody came in to talk to us. In fact, nobody ever came. We just sat there asking each other, "What's going on here?" They had us sit there until 10:30 and then said, "OK, you can go now." What was this, maximum security? I thought it was typical of the way the coaches treated us: as children, as guys who couldn't be trusted to get a good night's sleep, as a Junior B team you've got to keep on a leash instead of the professionals we were. Hey, we'd given up two months of our vacation to play. We wanted to be there. We weren't going to escape.

The big game came and the coaches couldn't decide who they wanted in goal. Our goaltending wasn't all that great that year anyway. Two coaches wanted Don Edwards, two wanted Mike Liut from the Blues. Edwards was probably playing better at that time, but they never could decide. They eventually picked Liut and, untypically, he played a brutal game. We were losing 1–0 after the first period, but we could've been and should've been ahead. Tretiak was his own remarkable, unbeatable self and he never let us back in it after that. What made Tretiak tough was his sheer size. He was quick and monstrous. He was nearly the size of the net itself. And what made it worse, he never left it.

I played so badly they should have sent me to Siberia. I gave away goals left and right. For some reason, I was stuck in mud. I was on a line with Guy Lafleur and Gil Perreault and those guys flew by me like I was a road sign.

My personal friend, Tretiak, had my number. I couldn't have gotten a puck past him if he'd been guarding the Zamboni gates. Plus, the Soviets' second and third lines were so much faster than us. What was weird was that it wasn't their superstars Sergei Makarov and Vladimir Krutov who beat us as much as it was one of their second-liners, Sergei Shepelev. He was incredible in the final game. He beat guys to the outside on two goals. I got zilched and we got hammered, 8–1.

Naturally, our loss caused the Canada Cup people to freak out. We weren't *supposed* to lose, so they changed the rules. They said, "Uh-oh, we need more than one game to beat the Soviets." So they changed it to best of three in the finals.

And the worst part was still to come, believe it or not. As they're handing us our plane tickets out of town, they finally got around to mentioning that there was a luncheon that day with the Prime Minister of Canada. How nice of you to tell us. Everybody had planes to catch, so most guys couldn't go. Only three went: me, Larry Robinson, and Butch Goring. I don't think I've ever been to a more embarrassing event in my life. Here's the Prime Minister sitting at a table set for thirty guys and three of us show up.

I was so depressed and embarrassed by the whole thing I went to Florida and hid in a condo for five days. My parents didn't even know where I was.

Not only had I let down my country, but I'd started people asking all those stupid questions about me again. "Yeah, he can score against the Winnipegs of the world, but what happens to him in the *biiiiiig* games?" I knew I'd spend the 1981–82 season trying to prove that my Canada Cup series was a fluke . . . instead of the other way around.

I decided the best way to do that was to change my style. I'd been passing ninety percent of the time. I was too predictable. Every time I'd come down the line, they'd play me to pass, not shoot. The pass was getting too tough and the shot too easy to pass up. Now I decided to try shooting more.

But even before the new season began, something terrific happened. In the 1981 entry draft, we picked the man who I think was the best goaltender who ever lived, Grant Fuhr. You can have Ken Dryden and Tony Esposito and all of them. If we had to play one game for everything I owned against everything you owned, I'd pick Grant. Everybody called him "Cocoa" because that's what he said he'd always been called. I just called him a lifesaver. When the pressure was on, when it was 4–4 late or 5–5, he'd close the door. He was a quiet guy, kept to himself, but he won more 6–5 games than anybody in history. He was hard as kryptonite when it counted. Unlike every other goalie I've ever met, Grant was absolutely unafraid of the puck. In practice, he wanted to stop every shot. If you scored on Grant, he'd give you a look to kill.

Everybody knows Fuhr was the first black goaltender in the NHL, but I wasn't personally aware of any racism toward him, certainly not on the team. There was only one time when his color even came up. The team was playing softball and we knew he was coming out so each of us put black greasepaint under our eyes the way baseball players do. But when Grant came, we handed him white shoe polish. He laughed.

If I'd had to face Cocoa for eighty nights, I'd never have set any records. I'd probably be working for Bell Canada, like my dad. But as it was, I found myself on a royal tear that year. By the thirteenth game, I'd scored thirteen goals. Then I got four against Quebec in the fourteenth and all of a sudden, people were asking me about the possibility of breaking Phil Esposito's all-time record of seventy-six. No chance, I said to them. Maybe, I said to myself.

After thirty-five games, I had thirty-eight goals, which meant that in an eighty-game season, I had a chance, although the pucks get bigger and the net smaller as the season wears on. But right then, just before the All-Star break, all heaven broke loose. Pucks just started going into the net on their own. I'd tip 'em in, bounce 'em in, wobble 'em in, elbow 'em in, wish 'em in. No matter what I tried, they kept finding their way past goaltenders.

In one stretch of four games I got ten goals — three against Minnesota, two against Calgary, one against Vancouver, and four against L.A. Now I had forty-five goals in thirty-eight games. In the history of the National Hockey League, nobody had ever gotten fifty goals in less than fifty games. All I needed was five more in the next eleven games and I would break the record.

We had Philadelphia that next night at home, December 30, 1981, and as I was driving to the game with one of our wingers, Pat Hughes, I suddenly got the strangest feeling. "Geez, Pat, I feel weird," I said. "I might get a couple tonight."

I don't get many premonitions, but when I do, I believe in them. When you've been as lucky as me your whole life, you pay attention to stuff like that. That night turned out to be one of the greatest of my life. It was almost eerie the way things happened. In the first period, I got a rebound off the back boards and shot it wide, but it bounced off Philadelphia goalie Pete Peeters's leg for the first goal. The second goal, I swear, I still can't remember. The third I got on a breakaway slap shot in the second period and the fourth on a slapper from the right on a power play with five minutes gone in the third period. That was forty-nine goals. All I needed was one more goal and I'd have done what I'm sure most people figured was undoable, fifty goals in thirty-nine games. I'd have completely skipped the forties.

But then the magic suddenly left me. I had three absolutely point-blank chances in the last ten minutes and Peeters stoned me on all three.

I figured it was over, even though Slats was triple-shifting me. Luckily, we were ahead 6–5, so with ten seconds left, the Flyers yanked Peeters. The puck went off the side of our net. Nine seconds. Grant jumped on it, and as soon as I saw him, I took off like I was late for a bus. Seven seconds. Grant got it to Glenn Anderson at the red line. Five seconds. I screamed at Andy, "PASS IT TO ME! PASS IT TO ME!" At this point, hockey etiquette was out the window. He got it to me and ... three seconds ... I fired it past a sprawling Bill Barber of the Flyers and into the world's most beautiful net.

Next thing I knew, Messier was leading a gang-tackle on me. Brett Callighen dug out the puck and saved it for me, which I'll always be thankful for. As soon as I could get all those people off my head, I ran into the locker room and called my dad. Since he wasn't at the game and because there was no television broadcast of it back home, I just had to share the moment with him. It wouldn't have felt right without talking to him about it.

"Wayne, what are you calling for? Aren't you playing?"

"Yeah, Dad, did you hear?"

"Hear what?"

"I got it. I got the record!"

"Geez, what took you so long?"

Then Bobby Clarke of the Flyers came in and congratulated me, which I thought was classy as hell. That's Bobby. On the ice, he was as tough as it took to win. Off the ice, he's a gent. When I saw him, I realized I'd set a record that was going to be real tough to break.

Later, Barber told me he was thinking of throwing his stick, which would have given me an automatic goal. He said he wanted to be an answer to a trivia question: Who scored Wayne Gretzky's famous fiftieth goal in thirty-nine games?

I thought it was also fitting that Anderson got the assist. He'd set me up on eight of the fifty.

Naturally, as is my custom, I egged it the next night in Vancouver. Somehow, whenever I do something great, I look like a geek the next time out. After the game, the entire team went out for one of those nights that you never forget. It was one of those nights when it just felt great to be young, healthy and getting paid to play hockey. It was New Year's Eve, after all, so we all went to a restaurant and celebrated. We had about as many champagne bottles opened as we did players. Somebody sitting there must have thought, "Boy, if this is what they do after 5–0 losses, imagine how they celebrate wins."

When the hangover lifted, I knew I was gonna beat Esposito. Even I wasn't going to screw this up.

As I got close to it, it got pretty wild. Esposito showed up in Hartford where I got three goals. Then two nights later I got another in Detroit. All I needed was one more and everybody could go home. On to Buffalo and an incident that should tell you all you need to know about my parents.

The day of the game my dad drove the sixty miles from Brantford — without my mom. Everybody thought this was really strange, that on the day her son was about to break one of the biggest records in hockey, in an arena close to home, she wasn't there.

"Where's Phyllis?" somebody asked.

"Oh," my dad said. "She's had to go to Quebec for a Pee Wee tournament. Brent's playing."

Nobody could believe it, but that's the way it was in my family. One of our parents tried to be at every game. My mom always tells people — "Wayne isn't the only hockey player in this family."

So, in front of my dad and a packed house, we took on Buffalo and, although I had two assists I had no goals myself. I kept looking up at Esposito. I could see the look on his face: "C'mon, Wayne. I didn't pack enough clothes for this trip."

It wasn't my fault. It was Don Edwards's fault, the Buffalo goalie. He started pretending he was Fuhr or Dryden. He stopped me cold four straight times. Finally, Buffalo's right wing, Steve Patrick, misplayed the puck in his own zone and I kind of jumped on it and snuck in number seventy-seven lefthanded. All of a sudden, I got two more just like that. After the game, even President Reagan called me, which was a thrill. It was a relief to do it in my sixty-sixth game. Esposito had done it in seventy. I didn't want any Roger Maris asterisk hanging over my head the rest of my life.

What I forgot about in all the excitement was

that I had a chance to become the first guy to break the 200-point barrier, too. In fact, it seems like everybody had. Nobody had ever even broken the 150-point barrier except me and Esposito. Who ever thought about 200?

Even my parents didn't think it was much. With five games left, I had 199 points. I called them. "You guys coming to Calgary?"

"What for?" my dad said.

"Well, it's not every day your son gets 200 points."

They got on a flight and came out and I got four points that night, with the 200th coming on an assist to my old car-pool buddy Pat. The one hundred goals never came, though. I don't know if anybody can get one hundred.

Then a great year suddenly turned awful in the playoffs. All my individual achievements and our number one regular-season ranking in the NHL meant nothing to the lowly L.A. Kings, who upset us in the first playoff round, three games to two, in The Miracle on Manchester. The Kings! We had forty-seven more points than the Kings!

I'm still not sure how it happened except that I remember we had them down 4–1 one game and lost 10–8, and we had them down 5–0 in Game Three — it looked so hopeless that their owner, Jerry Buss, left the arena — and lost it in overtime 6–5. We still could've beaten them by winning the fifth and final game at home, but we stunk up the joint and lost 3–2, with my future Kings teammate Bernie Nicholls scoring the winning goal.

Terry Jones of the *Edmonton Sun* said it was the

biggest choke in Stanley Cup history and that we were all "weak-kneed wimps." I really objected to that. My knees are fine.

But I still think it was the best thing that could've happened to us. It was a cream pie in the face. We'd gotten too big for our hockey shorts. We'd beaten the Canadiens the year before and we'd stomped on the rest of the NHL during the regular season. We were young and obnoxious. We jeered the Kings' power play line from the bench when we should have been yelling for more defense. Our assistant coach Billy Harris even ripped us in the papers. He said we were "antagonistic toward opponents, officials and referees" and that our behavior was "a reflection of Glen Sather's personality."

Harris, of course, got canned before the newsprint was even dry, but he was probably right. We were trying to be the Islanders and we weren't the Islanders. We didn't need to be rubbing people's noses in it when we beat them. We'd never even been to a third round of the playoffs yet. We were twenty-one-year-olds who were acting our age. We didn't know until then the kind of preparation and will it takes to win in the playoffs. I learned a lesson, too. All those trophies and awards and records feel great, but you learn that the tingle goes away pretty quick when you fall on your face in the playoffs. The whole season felt sort of hollow.

That off-season was horrible. In a town as small as Edmonton, where's an Oiler supposed to hide? The calendar couldn't fly by fast enough.

Before the 1982–83 season even started I knew I wasn't going to have a year like the one before. Sather called me in and informed me he was going to cut my time down from twenty-six minutes a game to twenty-two. He said we were going to be in for a long battle every year in the playoffs and that I needed to save my legs. He was probably right. By my eleventh year in the league, I had played 144 playoff games — almost two extra seasons. It was the same thing that hurt Bryan Trottier of the Islanders. He played 174 extra playoff and exhibition games before he was thirty and it wore him out. I didn't know it, but I was heading down that same road. Sather was just trying to prolong my career. I wasn't smart enough to realize it.

Sather also moved Mess to center that year, which took all kinds of pressure off me. In fact, it helped so much I started the season by breaking The Flower's twenty-eight-game scoring streak with thirty. That's also about the time I found out that I'd won *Sports Illustrated*'s Sportsman of the Year award for 1982.

I think to this day that's the award I cherish the most because I had to beat out great athletes from all sports: Herschel Walker, Alexis Arguello, Jimmy Connors and loads of others. A part of the reason I got it, though, might have been that I was taking a big stand against fighting in the league. So what happened? The night the people from *SI* were there to present me the award I got into a fight with Neal Broten. I'd only had three or four fights in my entire career, but I picked the wrong night for another one.

That was also the year I got four goals in the third period of the All-Star game and won another car. Afterward, the late Pelle Lindbergh, who was a great guy, came up to me and said he deserved the car.

"Why?" I said.

"Because I let all those shots by."

Not as many goalies in the league were as thoughtful as Pelle that day, but 1982–83 was a good year for me. I got 196 points, broke my assist record with 125, and won my fourth straight Hart Trophy, which meant a lot to me. Nobody had won it four times straight, not even Bobby Orr. Still, I would've traded those records in right then and there for a championship ring. I wanted the Stanley Cup so bad I could taste the silver.

We started the playoffs by blowing Winnipeg away, three games to zip. They had a snowball's chance. If there was one thing we *weren't* going to screw up this time, it was that first playoff series. Then we clobbered Calgary, our hated neighbor to the south. I played as well as I can play and Mess never played better. That was the first year he got fifty goals. Jari Kurri and I were almost telepathic, Grant boarded up the goal and the whole team was really rolling.

The poor Chicago Blackhawks could tell you about it. We played them next and wiped them out four straight. We scored goals against them just getting off the bus. One night we scored on our first five shots, then we came out the next night and scored on our first four. In all, we had twenty-one goals.

So, here was our chance: the Stanley Cup finals against the three-time defending champion New York Islanders. Here was our chance to bring the Cup back home to Canada. Here was our chance to end their era and start our own. Here was our chance to prove we weren't a preschool disguised as an NHL hockey team.

We got swept, four–zip. I contributed almost nothing: no goals, four assists.

We never had a chance. In Game One, with Bossy out with food poisoning, we hit the post four times. In Game Two, Bossy was back, but we still lost 6–3. That was the game when their goalie, Billy Smith, slashed me with his stick on the thigh so bad that I had to leave the game in the third period. Billy doesn't like anybody near the crease. In Game Three, Smith used his stick for other purposes, like to block every shot we tried. And in Game Four, they got three goals in the first two minutes and we spent the rest of the night wondering what our consolation speech was going to sound like.

Their big four — Bossy, Trottier, Potvin and Smith — danced all over us. Smith especially. He slashed, dove, screamed, whatever it took. He was so fantastic they gave him the Conn Smythe Trophy as the Most Valuable Player and they should have given him two. We hated Smith and totally respected him at the same time.

After that game, I'd have liked to move to Fiji for four months. I knew what was coming. *He can't win the big ones. He disappears under pressure. He stinks.* And you know what? I was almost starting to wonder myself.

Kevin and I loaded up our troubles and our junk and made our way to the bus. We both knew we were going to have to walk by the Islander locker room and we were dreading it: having to see all the happy faces, the champagne shampoos, the girlfriends' kisses, the whole scene we both wanted so much.

But as we walked by, we didn't see any of that. The girlfriends and the coaches and the staff people were living it up, but the players weren't. Trottier was icing what looked like a painful knee. Potvin was getting stuff rubbed on his shoulder. Guys were limping around with black eyes and bloody mouths. It looked more like a morgue in there than a champion's locker room. And here we were perfectly fine and healthy.

That's why they won and we lost. They took more punishment than we did. They dove into more boards, stuck their faces in front of more pucks, threw their bodies into more pileups. They sacrificed everything they had.

And that's when Kevin said something I'll never forget. He said, "That's how you win championships."

5

Garter Belts, Mickey Mouse and the Stanley Cup

That next season, 1983–84, was painfully long because we *knew* we *had* to get back to the finals. It's like getting bucked off a horse. If you don't get right back on, you might chicken out altogether. We geared ourselves to going back from the minute we lost. Every day, every practice, every game was a grind. Nothing was going to be good enough until we were back in the finals and tried it again.

That was also the first year I was captain of the Oilers. Lee Fogolin had been captain for a lot of years, and just before the season started he said to me, "Gretz, I want you to have the 'C'." The Captain's "C" they sew on your jersey is sacred in hockey, and Fogey's decision to give it up that year is still one of the classiest gestures I've ever seen in sports. He could have kept it. He deserved to keep it. But he wanted to tell all the younger players that the veterans believed in us. He knew we were becoming damn good. He knew we had a chance to win the Cup that year. The Islanders were great, but they were getting older and we were just getting better. Fogey was passing the team, and the dream, on to us, the kids. Maybe that was the day we stopped being an expansion team and became a team that finally felt it had as much right to the Stanley Cup as anybody.

But this captaincy business was tricky. Up to that point the Oilers had, for one reason or another, traded every captain they had while he was still wearing the "C". Even one, Ron Chipperfield, was sent to Quebec on the NHL trade deadline while he was away from the team visiting his terminally ill mother. That one shocked us all, but it was also the ultimate wake-up call that, with Glen Sather, the team always came first. That's why when Fogey presented me with the "C" I thought twice about whether I wanted it. These days, the Oiler captain is Mess and Mess will never be traded. If they're ever going to preach any loyalty to the Oilers club, Mark has to be the guy they keep forever and then retire his sweater. I think Sather would quit before he'd trade Mess. Of course, I've been wrong before. Famously wrong.

I wasn't your typical captain. I was real quiet, never would say anything too bad to anybody. Mess shoots from the hip. He comes into the locker room and says, "Man, you're brutal tonight. Get going." And whoever it is, gets going. He wasn't afraid to kick a guy in the butt to get him going. I couldn't do that, so I tried to lead by example: practice harder than anybody else, play harder. I made it a point to take in every new kid for a couple of days until he got himself an apartment and a car. Slats taught me that.

Fogey's faith gave me more confidence. I felt like the leader. Maybe that's one reason I started off so well. I scored at least one point in the first thirty-one games of the season to break my old consecutive game streak of thirty. The problem was, my shoulder was killing me. It got pinched against the boards early in the season when Dave Taylor hit me from the side. Now it was starting to ache. I wanted to rest it, but I couldn't. No matter how much the shoulder hurt, the streak kept going: thirty-five games, forty. It sort of had a life of its own. By the second period of game forty-one in Minnesota, I had four goals and four assists — eight points — but I was so exhausted I spent the entire intermission on the trainer's table. I couldn't move. My shoulder hurt, we'd played late the night before and I was gassed. I had absolutely nothing left. I went on the ice for the last period but I could barely hold my stick.

Plenty of times I thought the streak was over. In game forty-four against Chicago, Tony Esposito robbed me with a glove save on a breakaway in the first period and that was my only chance the whole night. Their center, Troy Murray, was giving me fits. Murray likes to skate right in front of me, making it impossible for me to go forward. Luckily, we were ahead 4–3 and they had to pull Esposito in the last minute. With seven seconds to go, almost everybody in the rink figured it was over, including me. Just then, Murray retrieved the puck in neutral ice and tried to flip it past me to his defenseman, Doug Wilson. I managed to bat it with my stick. It bounced high, so I reached up and slapped it to the ice with my left glove, using my body to keep Murray away. With Murray draped on me, I got over the blue line and slapped it into the open net with one second left. Not that I was worried or anything.

Now it was starting to become a zoo. We had national media following us. Las Vegas even laid 500-to-1 odds that I couldn't make it eighty straight games. The way my shoulder was throbbing, those odds were good that I'd never even *play* eighty games.

We played game forty-nine in L.A., and my shoulder got mangled some more. We had three days off in Palm Springs before we had to go to Vancouver. Good thing, because I couldn't move it.

But when I got to Vancouver, real disaster struck: I couldn't find my lucky garter belt.

See, hockey players use garter belts to keep their socks up, and I'd used the same one throughout the whole streak. It got so beat up and raggedy that I had to use a dime in place of the button to keep it together. Didn't matter. I wasn't going to change it. Not that I'm superstitious. But when we got to Vancouver, I couldn't find it. We'd left it in Palm Springs. So they gave me a new one. I tried to tear it and mangle it a little so it looked like the old one and, reluctantly, I put it on. It must have worked. I got two goals and two assists and kept the streak alive. Unfortunately, my shoulder felt dead. Somehow I kept it going that night and again two nights later at home against New Jersey with a goal, sixty-one in fifty games.

On the night that would have been fifty-two straight, we were playing the Kings. Their goaltender was Marcus Mattsson. I'd always had good luck against him, but that night, Marcus Mattsson sucked up every shot I took. My only chance came when I hit Charlie Huddy with a pass in the second period and he missed a wide-open net. Charlie felt sick about it, but hey, I've missed many wide-open nets and missed them by two parked cars. Actually, I felt like thanking Charlie. The streak was over. I'd gotten sixty-one goals and ninety-two assists for 153 points in fifty-one games — exactly three points a game — and I was relieved I could finally rest. I sat out the next six games. Unfortunately, Jari Kurri sat them out, too, and we lost five straight.

When you look back on that year, we went 57–18–5, including those five losses. That was a great team. We had *three* fifty-goal scorers that year. Me (87), Glenn Anderson (54) and Jari (52). No team in history ever had three. Not only that but Coffey had forty goals himself and Mess had thirty-seven.

That was also the year I made a few thousand enemies in New Jersey. We beat the Devils 13–4 one night and I felt so bad for their two goalies, Chico Resch and Ron Low, that I said, "They're putting a Mickey Mouse operation on the ice. They better start getting some better personnel. It's ruining hockey." You'd have thought I'd criticized Miss Newark or something. The fans went crazy against me. To this day I go into New Jersey and there's still the occasional sign: "Gretzky is Goofy." I probably shouldn't have said it, but I was feeling so bad about the way we'd killed them and I liked some of their guys, Ronnie Low and Chico Resch. I made the mistake of trying to divert the blame from those guys, but maybe it wasn't my place to lay blame or divert it.

We started the playoffs in a walkover with Winnipeg, three games to zip. We had to go seven games to beat dreaded Calgary. Then we swept Minnesota in four. That night when we got back into the locker room, we all took one big deep breath. We were all the way back.

That flight home was quiet. They gave us the Campbell Cup for winning the conference championship and everybody looked at it once and put it down. It was sort of an unwritten rule on that team not to give that thing a second look. The only trophy we cared about was a lot bigger.

For me, this series meant everything. It was now or never. Everybody was calling me one of the greatest regular-season players ever, but they said I choked in the playoffs. Gretzky was a scorer, yeah, but Trottier was a winner. That hurt. The players I most admired in my life — Bobby Orr and Gordie and Jean Beliveau — had all won Cups. Was I just going to be some guy like Marcel Dionne, with loads of scoring records but no championship ring? That kept me awake some nights.

We feared we'd face the Islanders. They had beaten us in ten straight regular-season games. I didn't get a single goal against them in the last Cup final, and this time they were all hyped up about the "Drive for Five." What did we have? The Run for One?

We knew we weren't as good defensively as the Islanders. Our game was speed and skating and finesse. Our game was using all five people in the play. We knew the more we had the puck on offense, the better off we'd be. So we decided we'd go all out on our forecheck, cut the rink in half, and not give them center ice. We also picked up the centerman early and left the wingers to the defensemen. We figured Trottier couldn't very well get the puck to Bossy if he was flat on his can. Then again, we thought we had a great game plan the *last* time.

We opened in Long Island with a 1–0 shocker. Kevin McClelland knocked one in early for us and Grant made a save you wouldn't believe on a Trottier shot from fifteen feet out. It didn't feel like a win. Billy Smith pretty much shut us down cold again and we were starting to wonder whether he really had our number. For the eighth straight playoff game against Smitty, I'd gotten egged. If it hadn't been for Grant playing the game of his life, we'd have lost.

Game Two was worse. We got blown out 6–1. I went through shutout number nine — I didn't even have an assist yet — and in two games all I'd taken were five shots. And all the while the Islander crowd sang me the Mickey Mouse club song. They even had a joke about me.

Q: What do Mickey Mouse and Wayne Gretzky have in common?

A: Neither has scored against the Islanders in the Stanley Cup.

It wasn't just me. Paul, Jari, Mark and Glenn, none of us had scored against Smith. The guy had us totally voodooed. Still, we left New York with a split. And with the league's new playoff format — two games on the road, three at home and two on the road again — all we had to do was sweep them in Edmonton. Yeah, right.

At least back home we had The Door. The Door was the door in our locker room that led to the tunnel. We taped a lot of famous pictures to that door: Bobby Orr, Potvin, Beliveau, all holding the Cup. We'd stand and look at it and envision ourselves doing it. I really believe if you visualize yourself doing something, you can make that image come true. Sometimes I'd catch Cof practically staring a hole in that door. If they'd let us unhinge that door and bring it to the bench, we probably would have.

Game Three was won by Mark and Kevin plain and simple. First, Mark scored the goal of the series when he faked their defenseman, Gord Dineen, out of his jock and jammed in a twenty-footer. Then Kevin became the first one to really torture Smith. He came swooping in on him and instead of shooting on his left side, he waited, teased him with it and then shoved it in the other side. From then on in, Smith was a pretzel. We slaughtered them, 7–2.

The team was playing great. I wasn't playing half bad, but I still didn't have a goal in ten straight games against these guys. Even Semenko had more goals than me: one. The press was all over me. That's when our co-coach, John Muckler, took me aside and said, "Wayne, don't worry about scoring so many goals. Just be sure when you do get a goal, it's a big one." That stayed with me.

Basically, what the Islanders were doing was staying on me even after I passed the puck. That way, I was out of the rest of the play. I was thinking about that the night before Game Four when I remembered an old trick Gil Perreault used when I watched him as a kid. He'd wait just an extra half second before making the pass so that his body was in the right position to get a pass back. I decided to give it a shot. It had to be better than what I was doing.

It didn't take much time to click. In the next game, Semenko hit me with a beautiful breaking pass in the first period, and I deked Smith once and then beat him with a backhand. That felt like the biggest goal of my career. The slump was dead. We had a 1–0 lead and I felt like somebody had just taken a grand piano off my back. Semenko came gliding up to me afterward with his arms up and that devil's grin on his face. "Hey, Gretz! We're tied!"

By the end of Game Four, I was ahead of Semenko two goals to one, and we were ahead of the world champion Islanders three games to one. All we had to do was win one more at home and the Cup was ours. I wanted that last game more than anything in my life. I wanted it so much that in the locker room beforehand, I got up and made a speech. I'm not much of a speaker. I don't think I'd made a speech in my whole career there. But I had to say it. "I've won a lot of awards in my life," I said. "I've had a lot of personal success. But nothing I've ever done means more than this."

The next thing I knew we were up 3–0. I got two perfect passes from Jari and turned them into goals and Kenny Linseman got one. The Islanders were going so bad that they even did the impossible — they pulled Smitty. As the third period was starting I looked over at their bench and couldn't believe what I was seeing: Smitty on the bench, Bossy without a goal for the entire series (imagine that?) and Potvin and Trottier looking sick.

All we needed was to keep from having our hearts bust out of our chests for another twenty minutes. I remember I never once saw Slats during that intermission. He knew he didn't need to say a thing. He was probably polishing his shoes. Unfortunately, when we got out there again, the Islanders' Pat LaFontaine got two quick goals. Then Potvin had a dead-on chance to make it 4–3. But, thank God, Andy Moog went into his Kreskin act. He read Potvin's mind and stopped him. That got our heads back into the game. Dave Lumley got an empty net goal with thirteen seconds left to make it 5–2 and the sky started falling.

Streamers and balloons came down. So did tears. Mark was crying. You can imagine what it meant to him. He'd grown up in Edmonton. His father had played pro hockey there. A lot of unfair things had been said about his family, and yet here he was bringing the city its greatest glory. He was named the Conn Smythe Trophy winner as the Most Valuable Player of the playoffs.

Across the ice, I looked at Kevin and I knew how much it meant to him, too. He called his mother down to the ice. Kevin's father had died when he was little. And when she held the Cup as proudly as the rest of us, it was a great moment.

For Grant it was sweet, too. Not only individually, but historically. He was the first black to have his name inscribed on the Cup. For Slats, it was proof that his ideas worked. He showed that you don't have to start three monsters and fight every other shift to win. The Broad Street Bullies were dead. An offensive team *could* win the cup and Sather had just proved it, and changed the NHL in doing it. I remember that the writer for *SI*, Jack Falla, put it best: "The sleek shall inherit the ice."

For the fans, it was paradise. It was like growing up now in Charlotte and you see the NBA championship on TV and you see the championship trophy but you can't *imagine* it ever coming to Charlotte. Hey, Edmonton had only been in the league five years. They swarmed the ice and smothered us.

And there I was in the middle of it all, holding that Cup. You know, I've held women and babies and jewels and money, but nothing will ever feel as good as holding that Cup. For me, it made everything I'd done, worked at or been through all worthwhile: all the practice and pylons, all the critics and the loneliness, all the headlines and the doubters. I won it for my dad and my mom and the rest of my family and for me, too, I guess.

I was thinking about all that and trying to keep my stick from getting taken by fans and trying not to cry when I saw Brent. He jumped in my arms and I skated around the rink with him on my shoulders through the noise and the balloons and the Cup and the goosebumps and the flashbulbs and the wonderfulness of it all.

OK, so maybe I hadn't been the best big brother in the world. But how many big brothers can give you a ride like that?

Afterwards, Slats made the mistake of telling us, "You earned the Cup, you do what you want with it." And so we did. Guys took it to bars and drank out of it. Guys carried it around the street, put it in their front seat, took it to their parents' house and posed every kid in the neighborhood around it. We took it to hospitals and plopped it down on sick kids' beds. I even saw a picture of one of the guy's dogs eating out of it.

I guess maybe that sounds sort of sacrilegious, but you've got to understand, the Cup is a symbol of the championship and once you can actually *hold* the championship, you want to touch it, feel it, use it, show it around. You want to relish the fact that it's real, it's in your hands, that you really *are* the best in the world. You want to let the fans feel it too, as a present to them. It was our way of saying, "Thanks for supporting us."

Personally, I liked to just look at it. Did you know there's a couple of mistakes on it? The 1963 Maple Leafs are spelled "Leaes," and Peter Pocklington put his dad's name on it and the NHL didn't allow it, so if you look closely you'll see all these x's through the name.

I love that cup. And even though we all knew where it had been we still wanted to have a drink out of it. Some germs you *want* to catch.

6

Yours Truly

Winning that first Stanley Cup changed our lives.

Suddenly instead of just the fans in Edmonton we had fans all over the continent, stories about us began to appear everywhere, and we were recognized on the streets and in restaurants in other cities. It was a thrill, of course, but some of us began to miss the days when we could meet people who didn't think they knew all about us already. I was tempted to surprise them with a few things they didn't know.

For example, hockey wasn't even my favorite sport when I was growing up. I always wanted to become a professional baseball player. I always dreamed of being a Detroit Tiger because Detroit was just a few hours from Brantford. I loved Mickey Lolich. Ferguson Jenkins of the Cubs was another hero, like he was to every kid in Canada, because he was one of the few Canadians in the majors. I was a pitcher — when the backyard rink melted, a pitching mound went up — and my specialties were the split-finger fastball and the knuckleball. I guess I was about ten years ahead of the split-finger craze, but my hands were too small to throw anything else. I was pretty decent too. I don't know if I'd ever have been good enough to play in the majors, but I did hit .492 with a semipro league in Brantford one summer. The Toronto Blue Jays even offered me a tryout once.

Another thing I'd tell about is my fear of flying. Just count how many times I've been on a jet while it's taking off or landing and that's about how many times I've wished I'd taken up another profession. I'm better now, but for a while there, I was one of the worst frequent fliers in the history of pro sports.

My problem with flying started when I was fifteen years old playing Junior A hockey in The Soo. Since The Soo was so far from everybody else, we constantly had long flights in rickety little DC-3s. One time we were coming in real late into a snowstorm and all of a sudden they woke us up to tell us to get our life vests on because we were going to make a water landing. It didn't happen, but it did scare me half to death.

Then there was the time that it was so foggy we hit the tops of the trees. Another time, I opened my eyes to find our plane surrounded by fire trucks, foaming us down.

It didn't get any better when I joined the Oilers. My first mistake was sitting next to our play-by-play announcer, Rod Phillips. He was a worse flyer than I was. Just before takeoff, he'd start rubbing the seat and his knuckles would get all white. Pretty soon, I'd start worrying, too. He ended up getting better. I got worse.

My phobia was at its absolute worst around 1985. I was in New York and I had to get to Montreal to play in my buddy Kevin Lowe's golf tournament. Four of us were boarding the flight and it suddenly hit me that nothing was going to get me on that plane. I just freaked, started sweating and getting jumpy and mumbling things, sort of like Dustin Hoffman in *Rainman*. So my agent and manager, Mike Barnett, got me out of there. We rented a limousine, got five videotapes and three six-packs and took an eight-hour ride to Montreal.

It got so bad that one time, flying in from Quebec City, they had to physically lie on me to calm me down. I was shivering so much they had to put a blanket on me, yet I was sweating so much I ruined my clothes. I was speaking at a banquet that night, so we had to borrow clothes once we got there. When I got up to the podium, I looked like I was homeless.

In those days I would do anything not to fly. Sometimes, when I was in Edmonton and we'd play Calgary, Mike and I would drive the three hours to Calgary instead. I always worried about his car breaking down. I kept seeing the headlines: GRETZKY HITCHHIKES TO GAME 5: CREDITS PLUMBER IN '57 PICKUP.

I tried everything to beat my fear of flying. I even

tried a hypnotherapist. We met him at 7:00 A.M. and went in his back door. We didn't need any more publicity about this thing than we were already getting. Everybody said this guy was very good. Mike Barnett came with me and the guy sat me down in a chair. He had me stare at the diamond in my ring for a long time as he talked. Pretty soon, the ring started spinning, just like in the movies. I don't remember a thing after that, but Mike tells me my chin just hit my chest and I was out. Then the guy began asking me about my past history of flying. It turns out I had all these stored-up incidents that I had blocked out of my memory. I told him how we barely missed another plane once on takeoff in juniors. And another time, I recalled landing in Atlanta and nearly hitting another one. He told me that from then on, I should sit with my hands on my knees on planes, look at the ring and think about how comfortable I was. It sounded great, but it only worked for about a month and then I was as bad as ever.

I took mind-control classes — until they wanted us to walk over hot coals. Nope. Finally, on one flight, a pilot snuck me up into the cockpit to show me all the buttons and gears and exactly how it all works. For some reason, that really helped. It made me feel safer. Now, sometimes when I fly a Canadian airline (the U.S. airlines won't let you do it), I sit in the cockpit during the flight and I feel more relaxed.

I finally got much better at flying during the trade from Edmonton to the L.A. Kings. Just before the deal was finalized, Bruce McNall said to me,

"Look, before I make this trade, you should think about the travel that we're gonna do here. Los Angeles is a long flight from a lot of places. If you don't think you can handle it, you can probably go to the east or Detroit, some place where you won't have to travel as much."

And I knew right then I wanted to come to L.A. so bad I was going to beat it. And I did.

Now if you see me on the plane, I won't look scared out of my mind, but I will look different than you might think. In fact, the first thing you'll say is, "You're so small!" I don't look much like a pro athlete. I'm about 5'11", 165 or 170. I look more like the guy who bags your groceries at the local supermarket. Some people think you've got to be 6'3", 250 to play professional sports. It's not so true of hockey, but even so I've always wished I were bigger, always wished I looked a little tougher on the ice, like Rocket Richard, with those black eyes staring a hole in your chest. My face is kind of narrow, so it makes my helmet look two sizes too big. I don't have big old Sequoia arms like Gordie Howe. Mine look more like toothpicks. I'm skinny. Somebody once said I could fit in a McDonald's straw. I can't skate at the speed of sound like Paul Coffey. I don't have the Slap Shot of Death like Bobby Hull. I don't click in my teeth in the morning and go banging into the corners. The way I see it, corners are for bus stops and stamps.

We took individual strength and stamina tests on the Oilers two times a year, every year. I always finished dead last. I had the worst peripheral vision on the team. My flexibility was the worst and my strength was the worst. My bench press is 140.

Because I don't look too mean, people are always trying to figure out how in the world I've done so well. Some scientist even theorized that my motor neurons fire faster than most people's — and we all know how painful that can be — and therefore I'm one fraction of a second ahead of everybody else on the ice. Some say I have a "sixth sense." People are always telling me, "You must have eyes in the back of your head," or "You just seem to be two seconds ahead of everybody else on the ice." Baloney. I've just learned to guess what's going to happen next. It's anticipation. It's not God-given, it's Wally-given. He used to stand at the blue line and say to me, "Watch, this is how everybody does it." Then he'd shoot a puck along the boards and into the corner and then go chasing after it. Then he'd come back and say, "Now, this is how the smart player does it." He'd shoot it into the corner again, only this time he cut across to the other side and picked it up over there. Who says anticipation can't be taught?

It was something he taught me every day. On the way to hockey games in The Blue Goose, he'd quiz me . . .

Him: "Where's the last place a guy looks before he passes it?"

Me: "The guy he's passing to."

Him: "Which means."

Me: "Get over there and intercept it."

Him: "Where do you skate?"

Me: "To where the puck is going, not where it's been."

Him: "If you get cut off, what are you gonna do?"

Me: "Peel."

Him: "Which way?"

Me: "Away from the guy, not towards him."

And on and on for miles. I had them all memorized.

My dad taught me a million things, like, to practice stick-handling in the summers with a tennis ball. Even as a pro I still do it. Using a tennis ball is how I learned to bat pucks out of the air so well. And because I can swat pucks out of the air, it's easier to hit me with a long pass. And long passes get you a lot of breakaway goals.

In practice, I try weird things. Guys will say, "You'll never do that in a game." True, but once in a while, something will work. I learned to bounce passes off the side of the net in practice. A defenseman could be between me and my teammate and I learned you can still get it to him by bouncing it off the side of the net. I practiced it so much I can do it now in any direction. Why not? It's legal. It's the same with the sideboards. People say there's only six men on the ice, but really, if you use the angle of deflection off the board, there's seven. If you count the net, that's eight. From the opening face-off, I always figure we have 'em, eight-on-six.

The craziest thing I ever tried was against St. Louis' goaltender, Mike Liut. I was stuck behind the net. There were two defensemen on either side of me and yet they weren't coming to get me. All I could do was flip the puck over the net, off Liut's back and into the goal. Boy, was Liut surprised. I

kind of felt bad about it, but it was either that or
stand back there until the ice melted. That same
night I scored not once but twice off the faceoff.
It's still the only two times as a pro that I've done it.

I love going behind the net, but I didn't invent it.
Bobby Clarke of the Philadelphia Flyers did it first.
The first time I tried it I was fourteen, playing nine-
teen- and twenty-year-olds in Junior B. It was the
Phil Esposito era when everybody wanted these
guys the size of condominiums to stand in the slot.
I got knocked over so many times in front of the
net that my coach, Gene Popeil, told me to try playing behind it. The net is like having another man
back there protecting you. You can use it as a pick.
If a guy chases you, you go out the other side. If
two guys flank you on either side, you flip it to
somebody coming to the net. If nobody goes with
you, you stick it in the goal and go sit on the bench.
I remember one night against Hartford, they must
have decided before the game that they weren't
going to come back there after me, come hell or
high water. They were going to stop me from passing, but not go after me. So the first time I went
back there, I must have stood there for twenty seconds. It almost became comical. I could've stood
back there for two minutes, I suppose. I could've
stopped and taken a sip out of the goalie's water
bottle. Finally, I flicked it out to somebody in the
slot and he scored. That position is hell on the
goalie, unless he really does have eyes in the back
of his head.

Not that I care much about goalies. It's funny,
but when I'm on the ice, I can barely see the goalie.

It's an attitude. If you ask a fifty-goal scorer what the goalie looks like, he'll say the goalie's just a blur. But if you ask a five-goal scorer, he'll say the goalie looks like a huge glob of pads. A five-goal scorer can tell you the brand name of the pad of every goalie in the league. I'm seeing the net, he's seeing the pad.

I get a kick out of people who ask me if I have a favorite spot where I like to beat the goalie. Paul Coffey, when he was with the Oilers, used to kid me about that. I'd come back to the bench after making a goal and he'd pretend to have a microphone and say, "Looks like you were going for just right of the kneecap there, eh, Gretz?"

"That's right, Paul," I'd say tongue-in-cheek. "But I had to turn the puck on its side that time. It was a real small hole."

I do like to do one thing to goaltenders. I like to wait them to death. I refuse to panic. Hold the puck, hold it longer, hold it some more. That drives 'em into a frenzy. They can't help but guess you're about to shoot it and lean just a little one way and that puts them off balance and, flick, you go the other way, just like my dad always taught me.

I learned how to count down the seconds on a clock without looking. From thirty seconds on down, I'm almost perfect. Most guys panic and make a bad pass or a bad shot thinking they're out of time. Thirty seconds is a long time.

I respect my traditions. I never vary. I get dressed the exact same way every day: Left shin pad, left outer pad, then right, same order, left sock, hockey sock, shin pad, then pants, then left skate, right skate, shoulder pads, then left elbow pad, right elbow pad, sweater, tuck the right side in, go out on the ice for warmups, *always* miss the first shot wide right, come in after the warmups, have a Diet Coke, an ice water, a Gatorade, then another Diet Coke.

I am always the first guy on the ice, after the goalie, going out for the start of each period. Unless my old teammate, Dave Semenko, wasn't in the lineup for some reason, in which case I was always last. I refuse to get a haircut on the road because the last time I did, we lost. I refuse to fly on Friday the 13th, for obvious reasons. Don't ask me why I do these things.

When I won *Sports Illustrated*'s Sportsman of the Year award in 1982, my hair was the longest it has ever been. That's because I was on a consecutive points streak and I couldn't cut it.

Right before a game — and I know this sounds weird — I eat like a prisoner. I play best on four hot dogs, oozing in mustard and onions. (Maybe because no defenseman wants to get near me after that.) I ate five hot dogs before Game One of our big playoff with Montreal, and got five assists.

For a game-day breakfast, I'll have two or three scrambled eggs with bacon, some whole wheat toast, coffee or tea, then a steak or some veal for lunch with some vegetables, a salad and dessert, and then, just before I go on the ice, I'll have a sandwich, a milkshake and a big piece of pie.

My training regimen is pretty simple: no weights, no running, no biking, no steroids, no special vitamins. In the off-season I work out with my wife to her aerobics tape (she does it with ankle weights on) for about forty minutes, play a lot of tennis, some basketball and eat right. That's it.

Long ago, Wally helped me figure out the biggest reason I've been so successful; I let the puck do all the work. People think that to be a good hockey player, you have to pick the puck up, deke around ninety-three guys and take this ungodly slap shot. No. Let the puck do all the moving and you get yourself in the right place. I don't care if you're Carl Lewis, you can't outskate that little black thing. Just move the puck: give it up, get it back, give it up. It's like Larry Bird. The hardest work he does is getting open. The jumpshot is cake.

That's all hockey is: open ice. That's my whole strategy: Find Open Ice. Chicago coach Mike Keenan said it best: "There's a spot on the ice that's no-man's land, and all the good goal scorers find it." It's a piece of frozen real estate that's just in between the defense and the forward. For a defenseman, it's hell, because he doesn't want to commit too far out and leave other people open. And yet, if he leaves you alone, you get a free shot.

Part of Wally's training was encouraging me to find my own tricks. I remember one of the reasons I always had trouble playing the New York Islanders was because they had the same color pants we did. I know where everybody near me is, but I do it by taking quick side glances without pulling my head up. You don't have to see a guy's insignia on his sweater to know what team he's on. You just need a split-second glance. But the Islanders' pants were so much like ours I kept getting them confused. My teammate Semenko thought I was kidding when I told him that. "Right," he said. "I suppose we could ask the Islanders to change colors." But it was the truth.

I'm big on using my feet. I try to make them as useful as my stick. Why not? Everybody's watching your stick and you can kind of skate past a pass like you've missed it and then reach back with your feet and hit somebody wide open. It's not hard. One time I did that when I was surrounded by four Canucks. I let the puck slide off my stick like I was losing it and then I left-footed it over to Jari Kurri, who just politely tapped it in for a goal.

I think I worry more about equipment than anybody in the league. My sticks have almost no curve. I don't have a great slapshot anyway, so I don't need a curve for that. And with a straighter blade I can stickhandle better and control my backhand better. I use one of the three heaviest sticks in the NHL because my wrists aren't strong enough to use a whippy stick. If it's whippy, I can't control it. As the season goes on, I use shorter and shorter sticks. By the end of the year, it's one and a half inches shorter than it was in October. I figure I'm getting more and more tired as the year goes on and that little extra lightness might get me a couple of pucks come April.

I baby my sticks. I tape them all myself and that's a lot of sticks. The night I broke Gordie's points record I used fourteen sticks. My blade is as wide as it can possibly be. I don't ever want to be one of those guys who is always saying, "Dang, the puck just barely bounced over my stick." Why let it happen? It's like the big tennis racquet — why would you play with a small one if the big ones are legal? I also never understood why guys would use white tape on their blade instead of black. The black is softer and thicker, which cushions the puck more. The only advantage of the white tape is that it's a little less sticky. But all you have to do is powder the black tape and you get rid of the stickiness. Before you can hope to develop any stick-handling abilities, you have to be smart with your stick.

You can blindfold me and hand me a stick that's a quarter of an ounce off and I can tell it's not my stick. It's the same way with skates. One time my boot-making company, Bauer, kept sending me skate models and I kept sending them back. There was something just a little bit wrong, but I couldn't figure out what it was. Finally, after I'd driven them all crazy with the seventeenth try, I found it. "It feels like I'm skating downhill," I said. Bauer checked into it and realized that the blade they were sending me was one degree steeper than the old one I had.

I've always skated in a very tight skate. I think it gives me more control. I don't want any slipping and sliding at all. I wear a size 10 street shoe but a size 8 1/2 skate. Most people's feet would go numb after about fifteen minutes, but my toes are double-jointed, so I can curl them up and not have it bother me. (Is this maybe more than you wanted to know about my feet?) At the same time, I want the leather to be super soft, so I can just flop my foot over one way and turn on a dime. If they're stiff, they don't give sideways and you can't turn as quickly. I just never could wear hard, molded skates.

My dad always taught me to wear the lightest equipment they make. It's a *feel* game and you can't feel the stick with riot gear on. So I always wear the lightest gloves and the lightest pads I can. I might be cold when I get in, but a few goals will warm you right up.

We talk a lot about referees, and I think they deserve respect. God knows they're underpaid and overabused. I'll argue with them, but I'll try not to embarrass them. If I do, I'll apologize after the game or I'll send them a letter. I've done it plenty of times. They've got feelings just like anybody else.

If you asked me, I'd tell you there are a few things I'd like to change about my game. I'd like to be better at defense, for instance. Cof used to kid me about it. He'd call me Flamingo, because when a shot came near me I'd put one leg up underneath the other trying not to get hit. And I wish my shot was harder, too, although I don't think you have to put a hole in the boards. You just have to be quick and bang it in there as fast as possible. Some guys have missiles for shots, but if it takes three months to load up and fire, what good is it?

I'm notorious for being no good at breakaway chances. I don't know what happens except that maybe I think too much. There are days when I can't beat anybody on a breakaway. One time, at a charity event, they had me going against a priest. Our trainer, Sparky, said to me, "You know, Gretz, you don't have a chance. If you score, you'll spend ten years in Purgatory." The priest shut me down. Then they had me go against George Plimpton, the author, and he stopped me, too.

I wish I didn't swear so much on the ice. I don't do it a lot, but I get out there and in the heat of the battle, I lose it and turn the air a little blue. The bad part is that my mom can read lips on TV. In fact, a lot of people, I've found out, can read lips on TV. To any kids out there who've heard me, I apologize. I hope it's not a part of my game you'll emulate.

Something that's always hacked me off is this lie that there is some unwritten commandment that nobody in the league will hit me. My God, when we played Mike Bossy, don't you think we were in the locker room going, "OK, you've got to run Bossy?" That's what they're saying about me, every game, I guarantee you. I've just learned how to make the great escapes.

Chalk it up to fear. When you're 170 pounds playing with 210-pound guys, you learn to find out where EVERYBODY is on the ice at all times. If not, you'll find yourself forechecked into the mezzanine. I mean, let's face it, if Ken (The Bomber) Baumgartner had ever hit me square, I'd be a smudge mark somewhere. Playing lacrosse as a kid taught me how not to get hit. I learned to roll with the checks so that you never get hit straight on. It's like when you go to one of those carnival shooting ranges. You learn pretty quick that it's harder to hit the moving targets than the ones standing still.

I remember one night in The Soo, one coach offered his guys $2 for each hit on me. They all figured they were going to cash in big, but as hard as they tried, all the guy ever paid out was $1, half a hit.

Still, it kills me what people think works against me. Neil Sheehy of the Washington Capitols was talking big one time about how he's "learned" to stop me. He says the way to do it is to deliver "rough body checks" to me. But the night he said that, we'd just beaten them 7–4, in Landover, and I had two goals and one assist.

At least Neil doesn't just cling to me like most shadows. I never could see what talent it took to follow a guy all around a rink all game, glomming onto his jersey or his stick the whole night. All I do is skate over to another member of the opposing team. Since my shadow comes with me, they now have two guys on me and that leaves wide open spaces for somebody else on my team. Shadows usually aren't too bright. If I suddenly went into the men's room, they'd probably follow me in there, too.

That's why I'm not ashamed to admit that I'll dive — pretend to be tripped — if I have to. Because half the times you're hooked, they won't call it. If you dive when the guy is hooking you and he gets a penalty, all of a sudden you're going to get a little breathing room. I mean, what else can I do? I'm not Mark Messier. I can't turn around and clunk the guy over the head like he does.

I understand that people consider me a great athlete and I appreciate that. But when writers ask me, "What does it feel like to be one of the greatest players in hockey history?" I don't know what to say. Well, a) I'm not sure I am and b) I just never think about it. I guess it's just embarrassing. If anything, I think about how to avoid being special. The last thing I want is a limo waiting for me at the airport while the rest of my teammates have to ride the bus. The last thing I want is the fanciest suite or the nicest table when I'm with the team.

It's like the time Gordie Howe was playing in the WHA. He was in his forties then, a legend, and he went up to the coach and said, "Did you run a bed check last night?" The coach said yes. "Well, why didn't you check my room? I'm part of this team, too."

That's the kind of thing I admire.

7

All You Have to Do Is Be Shot Out of a Cannon

It's just amazing how many companies suddenly want you to hold up their product after you've held up the Stanley Cup. I've done a lot of commercials since that day, but the best one I ever did was the one I didn't want to do. It was after the trade to L.A., we'd just had our daughter, Paulina, and my life was crazy. It seemed like I was doing an appearance every night. Usually my agent, Mike Barnett, won't push me to do anything I don't want to do, but on this particular commercial, he was all over me.

"Wayne, I'm telling you," he'd say. "You've got to do this one. It's really going to be great. You'll love it."

"Look, Michael, I don't want to upset anybody,

but I just don't have the time," I said. "Can't we cancel it?"

Ninety-nine times out of a hundred, he would have agreed. But this time, for some reason, he wouldn't. He finally called one night and said, "Wayne, you've got to do the commercial and you've got to do it tomorrow. It's now or never."

"Fine. It's never."

Naturally, I did it. Mr. Nonconfrontational. I had to get up early the day before a game and drive to a rented rink and the whole way there I was cursing Michael. "I'm gonna kill him for this . . ."

When I got there, the director said all I had to do was skate up to the camera, stop and say, "Bo knows hockey."

Bo knows hockey? You got me up at 6:00 to come down here and say "Bo knows hockey?"

Well, I couldn't get those three words right. Either I'd say it with the wrong intonation or say it at the wrong time or turn my head the wrong way or something. Sir Laurence Olivier, I ain't. Plus, game time was bearing down on me and I was getting antsy.

Finally, the director realized we had time for one last take or the whole day, all the rented rink time, the money for the crew, everything was down the drain and I'd be out of the commercial. So he said, "Look, just skate up to the camera and say, 'No.'"

So I skated up to the camera and said, "No," only I messed that up, too. I said, "No," kind of like, "No, I have no idea what I'm still doing here." And all of a sudden, the director jumps up and says, "Yes! That's it! That's perfect!"

Three months later, they sent the ad to me and I knew it was the best commercial I'd ever made. (Especially at the per-word rate.) As you probably know, all these athletes come on after Bo Jackson either hits a baseball or runs the football or dunks the basketball and they say, "Bo *knows* football," or "Bo knows basketball." But I'll tell you a secret. When they showed him "playing" hockey, what you don't see is that he's playing on a wooden floor in his socks.

See, Mike, I *told* you this was going to be a great commercial.

I'll admit, I've had amazing luck with endorsements and licensing deals. There have been Gretzky sheets, Gretzky lunch boxes, Gretzky wallpaper, Gretzky watches, Gretzky chocolate bars, Gretzky posters, Gretzky T-shirts and ballcaps, not to mention jerseys, videos, hockey games and even, yes, a Gretzky doll.

I hated that doll. Every arena I'd go to on the road, that doll would be hanging from somebody's noose. Or he'd be on fire. Or both. It came with a sweatsuit and a tuxedo, probably because the little Gretzky doll had to attend banquets. What they forgot to include was the miniature plate of rubber chicken.

We've gotten so many offers over the years — one company wanted me to endorse a softball glove for Pete's sake; what's next, a bowling ball? — that we now limit ourselves to long relationships with a few great companies. We're with the likes of Coke, Nike, Zurich, Peak, General Mills, and American Express. These companies have given me the opportunity to do some amazing things. For instance, I was in the first ever North American commercial that used a Soviet athlete. Tretiak and I were spokespersons for Gillette. We got nose-to-nose and pretended we were about to play in some huge, historic game and when the camera panned back, you could see we were about to play . . . table-top hockey.

People always want to know if I actually use the products I endorse. I do. I'm not a good enough actor to pretend. You'll never catch me ordering anything but a Coke, and believe me, people watch like a hawk to make sure. "You sure that's Coke? Lemme taste it." I'd hate to be stuck drinking something awful just for the money. For instance, I got involved in the concept, content and design of Pro*Stars cereal in Canada for General Mills, long before it became trendy to market cereals based on their health merit. They put my picture on the box. One day a kid came to my house in Brantford asking for an autographed picture. The only thing I could think to give him was a box of Pro*Stars. After he left, I realized I'd eaten half the box.

I can't imagine what Michael Jordan goes through with commercials and offers and speaking engagements and the like, but I know that there are some days when I'd like to unscrew my head and set it down somewhere and just forget the world exists. I remember one time early in my career, I'd been going crazy with commitments and we'd just gotten back from a trip to Russia, and my celebrity tennis tournament was coming up and the next day I was supposed to go to Toronto and do a Mattel commercial. I finally just told Mike, "Cancel it. I'll pay whatever it costs. Just cancel it."

They were furious. Boy, were they furious. But I just couldn't bring myself to smile for one more camera. So I took that day, went out on my grandma's farm, took a fishing pole and walked along the river by myself. You know I had to be desperate. I *despise* fishing. Mattel sent me the bill for all the wasted studio rental and crew members and it came to $15,000. And you know what? It was worth every penny.

I'm always being offered fees to go speak somewhere and have dinner. A four-hour deal, tops, and the money is well into the five figures, but it's worth it to turn it down just for the company of my wife and daughter and maybe a $2 movie rental. Some things don't have a price tag on them.

I get a lot of offers to do television shows, almost all of which I turn down. TV producers generally will try anything to get me on. One night I got a call from a TV guy saying he'd pay me $25,000 to be on his show. I got curious. What kind of appearance was worth that much money? It sounded funny to me. "What is it?" I asked.

"All you have to do is be shot out of a cannon," he said.

The truth is, money can be a large pain in the butt. I know you'd be glad to take my problems away from me, but when you have a lot of money, your problems go up with it. The more money you make, the more people want to sue you. And the more money you make, the more you end up worrying about everyone else. You don't want to be

Santa Claus, but you don't want to ignore someone who needs help. And believe me, I get calls and letters every day from people who could sincerely use my help . . . I think.

I still have the all-time greatest letter . . .

Dear Wayne: TV telecast a little story about you, your family, your career and your salary. They said you will get til 1991 about $50 million (my salary — $900). You are the only one who could help me. Eight months ago I have met a young girl and next year I would marry this girl, but it is impossible because I have so many debts (U.S. $16,250). COULD YOU GIVE ME THIS MONEY?? Could you make a present about the amount? Couldn't you? Or could you loan me $16,250? I would send you every month $50 til 2012. PLEASE, PLEASE, PLEASE. P.S. You are holding my life in your hands.

Sometimes it's not so funny. One time this lady called Mike, saying she was calling for Sammy Davis, Jr., and could I return the call? So I called and the lady says Sammy is in serious financial trouble and could I help? But as the conversation wore on, she finally told me that it wasn't really Sammy who was in trouble, it was her. She had a real sad story to tell. She was crippled and going to lose her house and all kinds of tearjerker stuff. I was feeling real sorry for her and started thinking maybe I could send her $1000 or so. So I said, "How much do you need?"

"Fifty-seven thousand dollars."

As it turns out, Sammy Davis, Jr., had never heard of this lady in his life. But it's hard. What I try to do is have some favorite charities and do as many events as I can for them. My celebrity softball sports classic in Brantford has raised over $1,000,000 for the blind. My father puts it all together with help from local business people, and we make sure that every dollar raised goes directly to the people who need it. Nothing goes to administration. I'm very active in charities for the blind because of a kid I met in an airport once. I was waiting for a flight, talking to some teammates, when the kid came up and asked if I was Wayne Gretzky. I knew something was odd, and after I said yes, I'm Gretzky, the kid said "I thought so. I'm blind, but I recognized your voice." Part of the deal for this book was that it be published in Braille, too.

Besides, what's there to spend it on? I'll buy clothes for myself and my wife, but neither one of us wears much jewelry. All I wear is a watch and a wedding ring. The house we bought in L.A. was too big, so we're actually looking for one that's smaller. We're not into buying $40-million van Goghs or anything like that. The only thing we like to splurge on is cars. I bought Janet a cream Rolls Royce Corniche for her wedding present. Me, I already had a black Bentley. But after a while, I got sick of driving around in something the Rockefellers would drive. It was just intimidating. I was driving home in it from Newport Beach one time and I realized I was so scared of getting hit that I was doing forty miles an hour. At that rate, I figured it was going to take me something like three hours to get home. So I sold that car to Mark Messier and bought something you could take the top down on — my white Porsche Speedster, James Dean model.

I guess a lot of sports stars spend their money doing drugs, but I've never, ever, not in my life, tried any kind of drug, whether it's pot, coke, speed, anything. It's something I'm proud of, and something I'll always be proud of.

Making money and being famous go together, of course. But I remember that at first it wasn't easy for me to get used to. The first time I was recognized outside of Canada was during Edmonton's first year in the NHL. I was on a plane leaving Chicago and the guy sitting next to me said, "Are you with the Oilers?"

"Why, yes," I said proudly, "I am."

"How many yards did Walter Payton get today?"

OK, I guess Nike wasn't ready to sign me up yet. But after that season I could tell my life had changed forever. It's funny, you live for twenty years being able to walk down the street, then one day you wake up and you can't do it anymore.

I remember being a teenager and seeing this gorgeous girl in a mall in Montreal. I got all my courage up, sidled up next to her and said, *"Tu es très belle."* You know what she did? She fainted. But maybe it was my accent.

I'd never been recognized in New York or Chicago or Buffalo before. Now, suddenly, I couldn't cross a street in any hockey city in either country without being stopped.

Nine years later, it feels weird if I'm *not* recognized. If I go in a room and nobody says, "Hey, there's Gretzky," it feels like somebody's playing a prank on me or something. It's almost a worldwide thing now. Janet and I went to Martinique once, just to get away, and we were walking down the street when we saw a kid playing street hockey with one of my Titan autographed hockey sticks. I just didn't feel like being recognized right then, so we ducked into a restaurant. Guess what was hanging on the wall? A framed copy of one of my *Sports Illustrated* covers. I had to sign it for the owner, a Canadian.

Actually, I love it. I don't ever have a problem with people wanting my autograph, wanting to shake my hand or to save my napkin or whatever. But it changes your life-style. Things most people take for granted there's no way I can do: grocery shopping, going to a mall, seeing a movie. I've tried going to movies and mostly I spend the two hours signing autographs.

You know what else it changes? Your clothes. I'm big on clothes, especially suits. I'll wear anything by Gianni Versace. My wife got me to go into this place on Rodeo Drive that specializes in the stuff. But I only buy dark suits. I stopped wearing anything white or light in public years ago. What happens is, people hold out their pens and markers in front of me as I walk and they get pen marks all over it. There's nothing more depressing than having a $1200 suit ruined by a nineteen-cent Bic.

The worst time to be famous is after a loss. All you want to do is get out of that locker room and kick trash cans. But I'm the one who's stuck, thirty minutes after everybody else, answering questions. I know it's my job. I never duck interviews. But I think I've answered more stupid questions than anybody alive.

"What's it *feel* like to have so many points?"

How do you answer a question like that? I've even been asked if my hair is real. Yes, my hair is real, but my teeth are not. Actually, six of them are not. When I was ten, a kid hit me with his stick and knocked out all my front teeth. My dad had just spent a pile of money on my braces and I'd gotten them off the week before. There, laying on the ice, was about three months' pay.

"Is it true you can't dance?"

OK, so it's true. I can't. Not a lick. My wife can't figure it out. "You have total rhythm when you're on skates," she says. "What happens when you unlace them?" Easy for her to say. She was Miss Dance America as a teenager.

Can I sing? I wish I could, but I'm tone deaf. One time, I was practicing this song I was supposed to sing on "Saturday Night Live" and I had my Walkman on with the tape in it. My singing was so bad that my own daughter, my own flesh and blood, started laughing. A five-month-old instinctively *knew* that it was awful singing. That hurt.

So many questions. I know the press has a job to do and ninety-five percent of them do it well. But some of them don't know hockey. Take Stan Fischler, for instance. He's got everybody in New York thinking he's an expert on the game. The truth is, he's not very knowledgeable. He once told me that I shouldn't take anything he writes seriously, since most of the time he was just saying things to rile people up. Fine, but when he writes something inflammatory, he never puts at the bottom of it, "Don't take this seriously. I'm just trying to rile people up."

The only thing that really irritates me about the press is that some nights I'll have had one assist and somebody like Luc will have had three goals and they come up to *me*. How does that make Luc feel? So I've made it a policy on nights like that just to answer questions about him and lay off the rest. That can make reporters mad, but so be it.

I know there are plenty of people out there who dislike me. There's even been an Anti-Gretzky Fan Club! Those people don't bother me. I get a kick out of them. I remember one time with the Kings, we got in a cab in New York to go to the game and the cabbie started knocking hockey players. "They're all a bunch of overpaid bums," he said. So, naturally, Bernie Nicholls started pumping him.

"Yeah, like that Gretzky guy, huh?" Bernie said. "He's pretty overpaid, isn't he?"

"Oh, yeah," the guy said, getting all excited. "He's a bum!"

The cabbie went on like that for ten minutes. When we got to the arena Bernie had him pull up in front of a bunch of kids whom he knew were waiting for us. We opened the door and the kids started screaming, "Mr. Gretzky! Mr. Gretzky! Can I have your autograph?" If that cabbie could've dug a hole in his floorboard and crawled through it, he would have.

The only thing that really worries me are the

nuts and the crowds. I never go out alone. I'm seriously afraid of being knifed. When you're out, sometimes people want to argue with you and if you're by yourself, they won't let you walk away. That gets a little creepy. We got up one morning in Edmonton and the front page of the *Sun* had this huge headline, GRETZKY KIDNAPPED? Janet and I just sort of looked at each other like, "We are home, aren't we?" It turned out the police had caught a guy who had kidnapped somebody else but wanted to kidnap me. He said he could have grabbed me, too, but he didn't because I was too high-profile.

The people who *like* you can be a little dangerous, too. I've had my clothes torn plenty of times. Once in Helsinki, Finland, they even broke down a glass door to get to me. I've been in cars surrounded by so many people that I couldn't open my door. I had to honk the horn until the police came. That stuff freaks Wally out. One time, we were coming out of a bus and so many people swarmed us that Wally was lifted off the ground and carried along in the crowd.

But, honestly, ninety-eight percent of the time, it's a huge thrill. I remember when I was twenty-two, I did an interview with *Time* magazine. About two weeks later, I was walking down the street, when I saw a drawing of me and Larry Bird on the cover of *Time!* The title said: "Simply the Best." I felt like doing a Mary Lou Retton double backflip. I took one to the counter, kind of hoping the lady at the cash register would recognize me as one of the guys on the cover, but she didn't. "That'll be $1.50," is all she said. When Janet made the cover of *Life* a few years later, I knew exactly how she felt. We have both covers framed and hanging at our house.

I've had lunch with the Prime Minister of Canada and the President of the United States. I got to the White House when I was twenty-two and we were at one of the All-Star games in Washington. President Reagan had done films about sports in the 1940s, and seemed interested in hockey so Gordie, who was there too, just chatted like they'd known each other forever. Me, I was petrified. I just shut up and tried to watch Gordie. Every time he picked up a fork, I picked up the same one.

I'm one of only a handful of people who've been painted by both Andy Warhol and LeRoy Neiman. I'm honored by that. Everyone talks about Warhol like he was this very strange guy, but I thought he was very nice. We did about a three-hour photo session and he painted from those pictures. He sold six original prints and gave one to me. Mike Barnett recently told me that mine has been appraised at over $50,000. It's hanging above my downstairs fireplace. I know that sounds pretty self-important, but it's a *Warhol*. Where are you going to put it? The bathroom?

I've met Muhammad Ali. First thing he said was, "Hey, you're not the greatest! *I* am the greatest! They call you The Great One, but only *I* am the greatest!" No argument here, sir.

Being famous has its perks. If I want to work on my golf game, I call up my friend Craig "The Walrus" Stadler. He gives me drivers now and again. Once, he gave me 144 dozen golf balls. Even I can't lose *that* many balls.

It's funny, but I've got all this money, yet people keep giving me free stuff. One time, when I was eighteen, I did an ad for a shaving company and they sent me four thousand razors. For a kid like me who didn't have much, just the basics, it doesn't seem right. Why give me my fiftieth sweat suit when most people don't have their first? That's why I give almost everything away. Do you have any idea how many travel alarm clocks I've been given for being on radio shows? I bet if I kept all the free tennis racquets and tennis shoes I've been given I could start a sporting goods store.

Hey, I'm not complaining. I never have to wait for a table, I get great service, and half the time they won't even take my money. But sometimes it's embarrassing. I can't ever use my name to get a nice reservation at a good restaurant. Either Janet does it or we don't go. I feel too stupid. A friend of mine was in town once and he wanted to take his wife to eat at a famous L.A. restaurant. Problem was, they said they were all booked up. "You call 'em, Wayne," my wife said. When they answered I hung up. I just couldn't bring myself to use my name like that.

The only other thing that embarrasses me is when players in the league treat me too nicely. One time, when Philadelphia goalie Cleon Daskalakis was a rookie, he told Sather, "When Gretzky scores his first goal against me tonight, I'd sure like to have an autographed picture." I guess the kid really wanted that picture because I scored on him in the first period. I autographed the puck for him and sent it to his locker room. I always hoped they'd trade him to the Calgary Flames so I could sign *a lot* of pucks for him.

I'll never refuse an autograph if I have time, but I can't tell you how many times I've wished my name was Bob Orr instead. That would have saved me months of time and barrels of ink. I've tried "W. Gretzky" but that looks bad. I can't understand why people want me to sign pucks. You can't see anything on a black puck. One time, a parent insisted I sign a sleeping baby.

Sometimes you can't win. I was eating dinner once with friends in Toronto when a woman came up and asked me for my autograph. I asked what her name was. I wrote, "To Gloria, love and kisses, Wayne Gretzky." About a half hour later she came back steamed. "How can you write that? You can't love me! You don't even know me!" She ripped up the paper, threw it on my lasagne and stomped out.

One time, our bus pulled up outside Joe Louis Arena in Detroit. That day there must have been a thousand kids waiting for autographs. I was dreading it. So my teammates convinced me to wear this big hat and big sunglasses and just walk through the crowd like I was a trainer or something. I did it and it worked! Problem was, my conscience wouldn't let me get away with it. When I was a kid, I loved autographs. So as soon as I got inside the door, the guilt just swept over me. I took off the disguise and went back outside and signed.

People come to my dad's house all the time in Brantford and want things. I try to keep a big stack of signed pictures there for him, so he can just hand them out. If I'm at their house, I'll sit at the kitchen table and sign for hours on end.

What's weird is when people come to my parents' door and want other stuff. Sometimes a busload of people will come and want a tour of the house. My dad will take them down to the trophy room and let them try on the jerseys and get their pictures taken with them. One time Wally was sitting looking out the front window when a guy drove up, jumped out, took a handful of grass out of our lawn, jumped back in and sped off. I get about seven hundred Christmas cards and six hundred birthday cards a year. Janet and I also lead the league in hand-crocheted baby bonnets. People just send us these things.

I get between two thousand and five thousand fan letters a month and we answer them all. Being famous runs me about $25,000 a year in stamps, colored photos and a secretary to answer it all. But there's no way I could ignore the requests, especially since my childhood heroes like Gordie gave me every autographed picture I asked for. I still have them, too. Now as part of my Coca-Cola arrangement, Coca-Cola gives us all the pictures and envelopes for free or it would be twice that.

I admit, I don't see every letter. I don't see all the letters from people asking for money because it would break my heart. I don't see the hate mail, either and there's plenty of it. The nut letters, people threatening my life, Michael sends directly to the police. One time a letter actually found its way to our house that was addressed "Wayne Gretzky, Kanada."

Fame is a big responsibility, and sometimes you

see more of life than you bargained for. Some of it touches places you can't imagine. I go to the children's hospitals a lot, and one time I met a kid named Derek. He was fourteen and he had terminal brain cancer. Still, he was real outgoing and fun. He asked me if I could get him some pucks, and I promised I would. I came back in a week with the pucks and a stick and some other stuff and I brought Janet, too. She signed autographs and pictures and she and Derek really hit it off. He asked me for one of my sweaters and I sent one.

Not long after, we were playing Pittsburgh at home. I accidentally got hit in the eye with the butt end of Jari's stick. There was bad bleeding and my vision was blurred, so I had to go to that very same hospital. After the doctor put a patch on the eye, I asked the nurses if Derek was still around. They said yes and wheeled me down in my wheelchair to the Intensive Care Unit. I knew that meant trouble.

Derek was just laying there and it was clear he was close to death. In fact, he died the next morning. He had so many tubes going in and out of him it was unbelievable. He had my sweater hanging next to him and my stick next to the bed and the pucks and Janet's picture on the bedside table. Janet was with me and as soon as she saw him, she started quietly crying and I was choking up, too.

All of a sudden Derek woke up. He looked at me and said, "Wayne, your eye looks pretty bad. Are you OK?"

8

Meet the Inmates

Someday, when I'm old and wrinkled, I know I'll be able to look back on those years in Edmonton and say, "God, I played on a great hockey team." Even though a few of us have ended up in other cities, the *parents* of the guys on that team remain close today. That's how tight we were.

It may have been one of the best ever. What memories we'll have. And I can still see all of them, like it was yesterday, sitting around in that locker room, sometimes quiet and determined, sometimes acting like crazy fools. I remember exactly where each of us sat. I was in a corner, with Esa Tikkanen, Dave Lumley, Dave Hunter, Dave Semenko (triple Daves), Grant Fuhr and Andy Moog along one wall. Mess was across from me with Kevin to his left and Cof and Glenn Anderson up from them.

I knew those guys well, and some people had totally the wrong impression of some of them. Take Dave Semenko. Most people see a 6'3", 220-pound monster built like a refinery and they shrink into the wallpaper. When I first laid eyes on him, I said, "I want this guy on my line so I can look after him."

People always called him my bodyguard, but that wasn't true. He was *everybody's* bodyguard. He was also a fine hockey player. The year we won our first Stanley Cup, Semenko played the best hockey of his life.

Semenko is also one of the most hilarious characters you'll ever meet. He was usually in hot water with Sather for something or other. I remember one time, he had been out at a bar doing those twelve-ounce curls he was so fond of and he got in about an hour after curfew. He sneaked through the back entrance, took the employees' elevator to his floor and figured he had it made. But when he walked in his room and turned on the light, there was Slats, sitting in a chair.

"And did you have a good night?" Sather asked him. It turned out to be a $500 question.

Semenko was far and away the greatest fighter I ever saw. He'd knock guys out with one punch and then hold them up so it didn't look so bad. Most of the time, though, he would just scare his opponents. He is just so huge and has such a wild look in his eye that nobody would dare test him. All he usually had to do was issue his famous line: "Maybe you and I should go for a canoe ride," and the guy would start backing off.

And if he didn't destroy you with his fists, he'd destroy you with his wit. One time Kent (Killer) Carlson, 6'3" and 200 pounds, started growling at Sammy like he was going to fight. Sammy looked at him with a little grin and said, "How'd you get your nickname, anyway, Killer? Did you shoot your dog?"

One off-season, Slats sent us all home with this fitness training package full of things we had to do, like doing fifty push-ups and fifty sit-ups and running two miles in under fourteen minutes. So one day Slats called Semenk and said, "You sound out of shape, Dave."

"I'm fine," Semenk said. "I'm doing the training program like you said. The sit-ups and push-ups are OK, but I'm having a little trouble with the running part."

"Uh-oh," said Slats, "is your knee acting up?"

"No, it's not that," Semenk said. "It's the wind. My cigarette keeps going out."

One time, I gave a car I'd won to him, just as a sign that I knew how valuable he was to me and to the team. His agent had ripped off something like $100,000 from him and he was having some money problems. Every day after that, Dave would call, wondering where the hell the car was. "I know what they're doing to it," he told me. "Some guy in Detroit is going, 'You mean Semenko's getting it instead of Gretzky? All right, let's take these leather seats out, yank the stereo, put on the bald tires.'" He finally got it — with all the options.

Now, over there, next to Cof, is one of the greatest rightwingers ever to play the game — Jari

Kurri. If Jari Kurri doesn't make the Hall of Fame, they ought to board the thing up. He is also the world's foremost expert on the TV series "Happy Days." Jari hardly spoke a word of English when he first came here from Finland, so the way he learned the language was by watching TV. He got hooked on "Happy Days." People said he and I could see inside each other's heads when we played, and that's true. Inside Jari's head are twenty-four-hour reruns of Richie Cunningham down at Arnold's.

Kurri has had to deal with some unfair rips over the years. One time Sather said, "A fire hydrant could get forty goals playing with Wayne Gretzky." Well, forget that. Somebody once calculated that Jari had a hand in 630 of my 1669 points in Edmonton. Without Jari, I'd still have been a good player, sure, but there's no way I'd have accomplished what I did. He and I just clicked on the ice, almost like we were twins. We had this little trick we'd pull. We'd be killing a penalty, and I'd go toward the bench as if to leave the puck there for the next guy. But just as it looked like I was going to give it up, I'd spin around and backhand a long pass to Jari, who was streaking down the ice. He'd slap it in. We scored more goals off that trick than you'd imagine.

He is a guy with tons of class, great breakaway speed, finesse, and a lousy right cross, just like me. Next to me, he had the most snug gloves in the league.

He was a great friend. I am godfather to his kids. Across the room from me is Paul Coffey, who ended up winning the Norris Trophy twice for best defenseman and also broke Bobby Orr's point-scoring record for defensemen, a mark that most people figured would outlast the League. Coffey has unbelievable skills and maybe more speed than any defenseman who ever lived. And the funny thing was, as fast as he is on ice, that's how slow he is off it.

Coffey was one of the guys I could be cocky around. I'd known him since we played ball hockey together when we were fourteen in Toronto. We could kid each other. I'd walk in for a game and he'd say in a real loud voice. "Wow, G-Man, those are really nice shoes! How much did those cost?"

"Four hundred dollars," I'd say.

"Wow, $400?"

"Yeah. Each."

Across the room is the goal-scoring machine himself, Glenn Anderson. He collected two things: racehorses and goals. Some guys called him Mork because he was a dead ringer for Robin Williams, but I always called him Andy.

You never had any idea what he'd do next. One time he got on a flight to Finland for the four-month Canadian Olympic team training camp and all he had with him was a shaving kit.

You could always set your watch by Glennie time — 15 minutes late. Sather would warn him, "Next time you're late, I'm gonna fine you!" But he never would. You couldn't really get mad at Glenn. Andy just loved to play in big games. The bigger the game, the better he played. If it was a Tuesday night in January in St. Louis, maybe he wasn't too up for it, but if it was April, you knew he was going to come up big. Andy had a far-away look in his eyes sometimes and you could just tell his mind was a million miles away. In the middle of a practice someplace like Winnipeg, Ronnie Low would holler out in the middle of practice, "How are things in Chicago, Andy?"

What people didn't understand about Glenn is that he is a terrifically bright guy. He was one of only a few guys on the team with a college degree (University of Denver), and his interests go about ten thousand miles beyond hockey. I didn't know until later how much time he spent working for the Cross Cancer Institute. He was always working with one charity or another. It'd be a Saturday morning practice — usually those practices were very short so the guys pretty much had the day off — and at the end of it, he'd say, "Hey, guys, can you hang around a little after practice today? I've got 500 kids coming in and I promised you'd be here." Typical bighearted Andy. And most of the guys would do it, because that's just how Glennie was.

I guess everybody knows how close I am with Kevin Lowe, so it's kind of hard to describe him. He could make a great politician someday, and I mean that in the best sense. He was always the best guy on the team to give a speech and make us all look smart. He was far and away the most well-spoken player. You always got the feeling that Kevin, more than anyone, knew that this was just a game we were playing and that the real world was waiting outside the turnstiles. More than anybody else in the organization, Kevin was the one ready for life after hockey. He's taken I don't know how many courses getting ready. He even worked for a franchise restaurant one summer to see if that was a business he wanted to get into. He was another guy who came up bigger and bigger as the games got more and more important.

There were so many great cogs in that machine. There was Dave Lumley, a true annoyance to everybody in the NHL and maybe the smartest player we had. There was Esa Tikkanen, another Finn and the kind of guy you loved to play with and hated to play against. He was either fearless or stupid, I'm not sure which. Tik could drive you nuts, he had so much nervous energy.

There was Dave Hunter, probably one of the greatest checkers and worst dressers ever to play the game. But he could hit hard. Hunts was a big old farm boy who loved his family. Here he was making big money in hockey, and yet every season he'd go home to help his dad bring in the crops.

There was Andy Moog, a truly underrated goalie. Only the players knew how good Moogs was. You could have stuck him in there for Grant in any situation and we'd have felt every bit as comfortable. One year, Moogs actually played more regular-season games than Grant, but when playoff time came, Slats kept him on the bench.

The little guy wandering around handing everybody towels and cups of Gatorade all the time was one of the guys I liked most, Joey Moss. Joey is the little brother of the girl I dated for seven years, Vicki Moss. He was born with Down syndrome. He's a great kid, loved by all the players and a big part of those teams. He'd work for the Oilers during hockey season and then for the Edmonton Eskimos during football season, folding towels, vacuuming and, mostly, just growing on you. He was a walking reminder for all of us. We players were given certain talents at birth and Joey had some taken at birth. Who's to say I didn't get what he lost? He was a symbol to all of us that way. He worked his butt off for us doing simple tasks that weren't simple to him and he never complained. How could we do anything but give our best, too? When we lost to Calgary in the playoffs in 1986, I was as down as I've ever been. Joey came over to me, put his arm around my shoulder and said, "Don't worry. It'll be all right."

Then there was our fearless leader, Slats, owner of the world's deadliest smirk. Semenko called it The Sneer, as in, "Uh-oh, here comes The Sneer." He had a way of sneering at you that would make you hate him for life.

Slats was some character. He could have been anything he wanted. Any job he'd have taken, he'd have been a big success. He was so good at investments that he was a self-made millionaire. He was always showing up someplace in a new Jag.

That was all part of Slats's power game. Since he was both the coach and the general manager, he got to negotiate contracts and he loved it. It was a replacement for the competition of hockey for him. If your agent wasn't well prepared when he went in there, Slats would kill you. One time, Semenko's agent, Peter Spencer, went in and Slats threw him a question about Semenko's plus-minus rating.

Spencer wouldn't know a plus-minus rating if it bit him. Slats kicked him out.

Slats loved trying to get the upper hand so much that he went over the line. He'd do sleazy things, like try to get a player to come in and do a contract one-on-one, rather than with his agent. Because he was the coach, too, some of the young kids would do it rather than risk making him mad. They'd come out of his office a lot poorer.

But you had to give Slats his due as the coach. He, along with Ted Green, John Muckler and our personnel director Barry Fraser, literally were changing the NHL. Until they came along, Philadelphia was the format for teams to model themselves by — big guys, power, fighters. That's how teams were trying to build themselves. But the Oilers were suddenly changing all that. The new way to go was speed to burn, finesse and loads of skill. We scored over four hundred goals for five straight seasons, an achievement that was unthinkable even three years before.

Who could stop us? Grant was twenty-two, Mark and Paul and I were all twenty-four, Jari and Kevin were twenty-five. It looked like we were going to build a dynasty. We were even making fans of some unlikely people. I remember after the 1983 Stanley Cup finals, I went to New York to accept an award from Seagram's as the top player in hockey. Seagram's was the most fun award to win because they'd fly you down to New York for three days and give you a beautiful trophy and a cheque. We went to a Yankee game, Mike Barnett, Charlie Henry and I, and a bat boy came up to us during the game and said, "Billy Martin wants to see you guys after the game."

Well, we didn't really know what seeing Billy Martin meant. None of us had met him before. By the time we left the locker room, we'd met all the players and drank beers until 1:30 in the morning. All I remember is Billy talking about how he couldn't believe Billy Smith had slashed me. The more beers he had, the madder he got. Finally, he stormed out of the locker room saying, "Let's go get him!" He wanted to head out to Long Island to kick his butt.

That off-season didn't last long. By August, eight of us were back at it, getting ready for the 1984 Canada Cup, with Slats as head coach. Slats was no dummy. He knew we could play together and it would give us a leg up on the rest of the league besides. By the time opening day of the NHL season rolled around, we'd be sharp.

That Canada Cup was anticlimactic. We avenged the 8–1 whitewash we'd taken in 1981, but it wasn't the same. My friend Tretiak had retired from the Red Army team. There were offers from other NHL teams to lure him to the U.S., but no way in a million years would Vlad have ever even considered defecting. He was totally Communist in his ideals and his beliefs. If he'd left at all, and he wouldn't have, the only team he would have considered was the Montreal Canadiens. To him, the Canadiens played hockey the way it was supposed to be played, like gentlemen. When the Soviets played the Philadelphia Flyers, the Flyers would run them, and Tretiak despised those kind of tactics. He felt like that wasn't hockey at all. But when the Soviet Red Army team tied the Canadiens 3–3 on New Year's Eve in the Super Series 8-game tournament, Tretiak told me he thought that was one of the greatest hockey games ever played.

Now that the Soviets' idea of Communism has pretty much been scrapped, Vlad might consider coming to the U.S., but it's too late in his career. Although, just to tell you how great he was, some NHL teams are still asking him anyway. If the Los Angeles Rams called, he might actually come.

The other way that Canada Cup was a letdown was that the Soviets didn't even make the final. We ended up playing Sweden in the final instead of the Soviets and there's no way, not in a hundred years, that the Swedes were going to beat us in Canada for the Cup. It was no contest. I'm not trying to blast the Swedes. Hockey there is improving every year and they absolutely love the NHL. Someday soon we'll have a European branch of the NHL and people will be surprised at how good the play will be.

But at that time, no way was Sweden going to beat us. Our toughest competition were the guys in our own locker room. There were six Islanders on that team and eight Oilers and it was like getting rival street gangs together for a prom. We'd spent the previous two years trying to cave in each other's noses and suddenly we were supposed to love each other. Me, I didn't even know there was any friction, maybe because Bossy and I never talked anyway. Finally, we had a big meeting. Slats saw what was happening and got Larry Robinson and me to call a team meeting. We all got together with a bunch of beers in a hotel room. Then Bob Bourne of the Islanders just came out and said it. "Let's face it. We just don't like you guys."

That was the turning point. That got everything out in the open. From our point of view, we didn't hate them at all. I could see where they hated us, we'd just taken their Cup away from them. But the fact is, we didn't hate them. We admired them. They had done what we were trying to do. We may have come off as cocky to them, but we were only cocky to hide our fear that we wouldn't be as good as they were. I told them that, in so many words, and we got over that hump and had no more problems.

On September 13, 1984, we played a great game to defeat the Soviets 3–2 in overtime in the semifinals. Or rather, Cof played a great game. It was 2–2 in the third period and we were sure that if we could get them into overtime, they'd lose, because they had never played overtime. Their system doesn't have it, and neither does the Olympics or the World Championships. We figured that in the high-pressure world of overtime, when one mistake can end it for you, they'd be clueless.

Shows you what we knew. In overtime, they suddenly got a two-on-one break, with Vladimir Kovin and Mikhail Varnakov bearing down against Coffey and our goalie, Pete Peeters. Was this two straight Canada Cups heading back to the Kremlin? Nope. The instant Kovin tried to pass, Coffey stuck his stick out and deflected the puck away. Then he picked it up, skated like a maniac back up the ice and shoved it into the corner where John Tonelli dug it out. John got it back to Coffey at the point. Cof fired a shot that Mike Bossy ticked with his stick into the net and we won. Not a bad play for a guy who isn't supposed to be able to play a lick of defense.

That was it. We went on to beat Sweden, were given seven days off and then it was back to the NHL grindstone.

Luckily, we came to familiar surroundings — people giving us no chance to repeat. *Inside Sports* said: "It's only a one-year dynasty for Gretzky and Team Arrogance." My old buddy Stan Fischler wrote this and I saved it: "Despite a few big goals (the result of conspicuously lucky breaks) Gretzky was mostly manacled by his foes and betrayed weaknesses. The Islanders subdued Gretzky in the finals merely by persistent checking." Then Rocket Richard came out and said that I wouldn't have scored as much "in the old days."

What did we have to do to prove ourselves? What did I have to do? I admire Rocket Richard, but Rocket Richard is still angry that Gordie passed him. In every other sport — the NBA, track, major league baseball, the NFL — almost everybody admits that performance is better now than it was twenty years ago. For some reason, though, hockey has a hard time keeping up with the calendar. Let's face up to it! The game is better now. The athletes are better and the competition is tougher. And it's going to be tougher and better ten years from now.

Anyway, those remarks got to me. And that's

when I decided that one of my goals (I never said it publicly) was to average two assists a game. I'd had 125 assists two years before; all I needed was 35 more.

The way that season started, I thought we were all going to be setting records. We went fifteen games unbeaten and in those fifteen, Jari had eighteen goals. Jari and I were playing for the first time that year on a line with The Krusher, Mike Krushelnyski, a moose on skates. Krusher had a bit of a hard time figuring out what Jari and I were doing at first. "I think I'm getting the hang of you, Gretz," he told me one day. "I only ran into you twice today." Krusher is 6'3", 210. You don't want him to run into you *once*.

I owe a lot to Krusher. Besides being a wonderful teammate, he gave me one of my best memories. On December 19 of that year, he took one of my rebounds and flicked it in to give me my 1000th point, a record that meant a lot to me.

By regular season's end, we were again the best team in the league, 49–20–11. Kurri broke the record for goals by a rightwinger with 71. I got 135 assists — a new record, but not quite what I'd hoped.

As the annual Cup chase began again, we realized something. The Cup is addictive. You think it's yours, and so you become like a selfish kid — you don't want anybody else to touch it, see it, have it or study it.

We opened by beating the Kings in three hair-raisers, two in overtime. Let's just say we were glad to get past them. Then wins over Winnipeg and

Chicago brought us to the Philadelphia Flyers and the Stanley Cup final. We hadn't beaten the Flyers in our last eight straight road games. Most people figured they had a lock on us. But if people would think about things, they'd be able to see through stats like that. Yeah, we'd lost a lot of regular-season games in Philadelphia, but that's going in there on long road trips. You get in late, get a lousy night's sleep and have to play the next day. In the playoffs it's a different story. You go in there a couple days ahead, get a lot of rest, play the game, get another day's rest and play again. I knew we'd do better this time.

Naturally, we went out and stunk up the Spectrum the first night, rest or no rest. Philadelphia never admitted it, but I think they purposely made the ice choppy to slow us down. It was like playing on a lake. We got lambasted 4–1, so bad that the next day Slats refused to even show us videos of the game. He just burned them. That was smart. We all knew it was one of our worst games of the year.

The next day's paper had an article by a *Philadelphia Inquirer* reporter calling me and the team a "fraud." I was so furious I was ready to play right then and there, 8:00 in the morning. Say what you want about me, but don't say our team has no heart.

Slats shook everything up for Game Two by putting Tik on my line with Jari. It was just what we needed, something fresh and new and it worked. We beat Philly 3–1, and afterward, Tik got The Shave, with Pocklington himself manning the scissors.

It was back to Edmonton and the same setup as the year before, sweep three at home and you win the Cup. We beat them 4–3 right off.

In Game Four, Philadelphia went up 3–2, but Anderson got us back in it with a goal and then Grant made the play of the series by stopping Ron Sutter's penalty shot like he had a magnet in his glove. It turned the game around for us and we won 5–3.

Now it came down to Game Five. Win now or drag our poor bodies back to Philadelphia for two more and no one, but no one, wanted to see the city of Philadelphia again. Nothing personal, Philadelphia.

No problem. We came out flying and squashed Philly. Cof and I hooked up with what may have been our prettiest play of the year. He had the puck in his end and flipped it across ice to me at about the red line. Then he just skated as fast as he could after me — all-out, head down, breaking-the-Coffey-barrier skating. Nobody I've ever skated with is faster than Paul Coffey. When I got to the blue line I flipped it behind my back to him, no-look. Call it telepathy or whatever, I just *knew* he'd be there. He never even looked up. My pass hit the tape on his stick and he gunned it in.

Everything after that was just waiting for the champagne. Ed Hospodar of the Flyers gave me a check that left me motionless on the ice for a minute. Finally, I opened my eyes, looked up at Hospodar and said, "Don't you know the score is 4–1?" He burst out laughing.

I won the Conn Smythe, but Cof deserved it. To

this day I wished they'd given it to him. He was the true superstar of those playoffs. He did it with a bad right foot, a strained back, a bruised right hip and probably a busted spleen or something.

Looking at Cof after the game, I realized how much we had come to look like those bruised and beat-up Islanders of the old days. And I knew then, too, that each time it gets harder. And I wondered who was sitting around their living rooms looking at us like we were yesterday's news, ready to knock us off our throne.

Swigging beer out of that Cup (we learned our lesson: champagne stings your eyes), I was thinking that we were sitting on the edge of one of the great dynasties in hockey. The Flyers were the only team that could touch us, and we'd just shipped them home on the early flight. I remember thinking, "This team could win five Cups in a row easy, maybe more."

Well, maybe not so easy.

9

Back to the Future

The day after we won that second Cup, the police told me that two people had threatened my life. They didn't want to tell me during the play-offs because they thought it might bother me. I didn't pay too much attention (OK, maybe a *little* attention), and nothing came of it. But maybe it was a bad omen. Maybe the whole team should have taken the year off.

That next season, 1985–86, started out so well. Everything was perfect. The team looked unstoppable. At the beginning of camp, Sather told all the draft choices and free agents, "Boys, you're competing for one spot on this team, maybe two." He wasn't going to give them the standard nobody's-job-is-safe-on-this-team line. He was going to tell them the truth. We were a tight group and Sather was going to keep us tight.

With Slats in charge, I always liked to think of us as the Oakland Raiders of the NHL. Sather wasn't afraid to take chances on guys who had been left for dead. Guys most teams were willing to sell for scraps, Sather picked up, polished and set back on the ice, where they played their hearts out. Kevin McClelland couldn't make it with Pittsburgh, the last-place team in the league. He came to us and really contributed. Marty McSorley was an up-and-down player until we got him. Pittsburgh had bumped him down to the minors. He was a star with us.

Me, I'd never felt better. I was twenty-four years old, making more money than I could spend, eating out every night, living the life I wanted and playing some pretty good hockey. That season I got fifty-two goals, my lowest total since my rookie year, but my assists were way up. I got my two a game plus change — 163 — and set a new NHL record with 215 points.

All in all it was probably my best year. I'm not trying to be a jerk, but I don't remember a single game that I didn't play as well as I possibly could have. Twice I had seven assists in one game — against Chicago and Quebec. It was maybe *our* best year, too. We ended up on top of the league again, 56–17–7, 119 points. Philly was nine points behind us, all of which is why what happened to us still breaks my heart.

Our first problem was Vancouver. They were too easy. We flattened them 7–1, 5–1 and 5–1. Gee, I hated to do that to my favorite goalie, Vancouver's Richard Brodeur — King Richard, as he's known. King Richard always told the press that I talk too much. I thought that was funny, considering I only said one thing to him my whole life. He has this habit, every time he makes a save, of skating out of the net about fifteen feet before he gives the puck back to the referee. So one time he did it I just skated up to him and yelled, "Stay in your (bleep) net!"

Anyway, we all knew we were going gang-busters. We'd just won two Cups and run away with the regular season and now we were going to walk through the playoffs.

On to Calgary, a team we'd never lost to in a playoff series. Just before that series opened, though, the Flames went and did something smart. They picked up John Tonelli from the Islanders. Tonelli, a hellacious competitor, gave them not only eleven years of smarts but a winner's attitude, the *knowledge* of how to win. The Calgary fans sensed something was different. They were dying to rub us out. They were dying to rub *me* out.

Then, just before Game One, Grant got word that his father had died. People think because Grant is so quiet that he's not emotional, but he is, he just keeps it inside. We were worried about him, but Grant wanted to play and Sather decided to start him. We got beat — at home, no less — 4–1. No problem. No panic. We came out in Game Two and Andy had to conjure up a magical goal in over-time to beat them, 6–5. And it went like that, neck and neck, splitting the next four games, winning one at home and one on the road. But we figured the worm had turned when we beat them in a fantastic Game Six in Calgary. All we had to do was beat them at home in Game Seven and put them on the next plane out of our sight.

Unfortunately, the Flames had made other plans. They got us down 2–0 late in the second period. Presto, we came back with two quick goals to tie it up and went into the locker room before the third period thinking, "Yeah, we're all right. Let's freeze them out, get us a goal and go suck some beers." But that's when IT happened.

Steve Smith was this big, good-looking defenseman of ours, only twenty-three years old, a future star, a Kevin Lowe protégé. He is a real smart player, but that night he made a mistake. He took the puck in our own corner and tried to clear it across the crease: *the* cardinal no-no in hockey. It's like setting a glass of grape juice on your new white cashmere rug. You could do it, but what's the percentage in it? Without a single Flame around, the puck hit the back of Grant's left calf and caromed back into our net. Hardly anybody in the arena saw it but the goal judge did. The Flames suddenly led 3–2. It was a horrible, unlucky, incredible accident, but it happened. Steve came to the bench and, for a minute, looked like he'd be all right. But then he broke down in tears.

We all figured we'd get it back. We had thirteen minutes to go and chances like crazy, five on their goalie, Mike Vernon. We missed them all. Time ran out on us. As things would turn out, that fluke kept us from winning a record five straight Stanley Cups. The date was April 30, 1986, Steve Smith's birthday.

Everybody wanted to blame Smith, but that was

a total cop-out. It wasn't Steve Smith who blew the opener at home and it wasn't Steve who beat us at home in Game Five and it wasn't Steve who let in the first two goals of that game, either. Steve is a damn good player and, in fact, he became a fine defenseman. Besides, maybe we were lucky to lose that year. I know that sounds strange, but sometimes you lose for a reason. After that season, we made some changes, got hungrier, and stopped thinking we had sole rights to the Stanley Cup. Maybe Smith *won* us two more Cups. Who knows?

Our head coach, for one, wasn't blaming Steve. He was blaming everybody else.

"I gave them a game plan and they didn't follow it," Slats told the press afterward. Slats was always a lousy loser, so rather than accept the loss, he bought out of it altogether.

When you give your respect to a coach, when you lay down to his authority and believe he believes in you, something like that hurts. All of a sudden, for the first time in a long time, we were down, and what did Slats do? He kicked us.

It made me feel a little better to win my seventh straight Hart Trophy, but not much. I wish I could have enjoyed it a little, but the world was saying the Edmonton Oilers had just driven themselves off the end of the pier. The papers really hammered us. But nobody nearly *ruined* us like *Sports Illustrated*.

Sather told us during the playoffs that a guy named Don Ramsey was doing a story on drugs in the NHL for *Sports Illustrated* and that nobody was supposed to talk to him. Nobody did. When the story came out, it charged that some of our players were heavily into drugs.

One of Ramsey's pieces of "evidence" was some picture of our guys holding straws in the Stanley Cup the year before. Supposedly, they were doing cocaine. They did have straws in the Cup, but they had them in there in order to drink the world's biggest B-52 shooter, a wild concoction of liqueurs and booze. See, they couldn't tip the Cup up and drink it like champagne because a B-52 has layers, so they had to drink it with straws.

I knew everybody on that team and I never saw anybody doing any drugs, anytime, anywhere. Never. The worst thing I ever saw in the locker room was Sudafed, a cold remedy available in any drugstore. Some guys claimed it gave them energy. Once the Oilers' coaches wanted me to take DMSO, an arthritis drug, for my sore shoulder and I refused. The stuff isn't even legal in Canada.

Anyway, nobody ever proved anything about drugs on us. In fact, nobody even came close to finding anything even remotely suspicious. But it was too late. We had a new image problem to fight. All of a sudden we were dopeheads who had taken a possible hockey dynasty and snorted it up their noses. We knew the only way to make people forget it was to start winning again. So that's exactly what we did. We added Reijo Ruotsalainen of Finland to our collection of great players from abroad and by the end of that next season, 1986–87, we had, once again, the best record in the league, with Philly six points back, again.

That year we took every single shift in those

playoffs dead seriously. The last thing we were going to do now was be overconfident. We got by the Kings in five games, Winnipeg in four and then Detroit in five.

The Stanley Cup final was the one TV wanted — us against Philly in a rematch of 1985. We won the first two games in Edmonton right off the bat, but not without some nastiness. In Game Two, Philadelphia coach Mike Keenan accused me of "diving" — pretending to be tripped in order to draw a penalty. He told the press I used "poor conduct. . . . You expect more from the best hockey player in the world," he said. "All he's doing is embarrassing the officials."

Part of the problem was that at that time Keenan hated Slats and would do almost anything to get under his skin. Professional tension, I guess. The other reason he did it is because Keenan will do anything to win. He's a lot like Slats that way, I guess.

Me? Diving? Sure I dive. If my defender isn't going to get called for things he's doing, I'll try to get him penalized for things he's *not* doing. But in Philadelphia I didn't dive. Lindsay Carson hooked me and I went down. A guy jams his stick between your feet, you tend to fall down, right? Next thing I knew Keenan was screaming at me, "Earn your chances!" I couldn't believe it. I had a real snappy comeback: "Pardon?"

Not that Philly's players were altar boys. In Game Four, with us leading the series two games to one, their goalie, Ron Hextall, who I generally like, took a swing right on the back of Kent Nilsson's knees. Kent went down and there was a penalty. We stuck it to them anyway, 4–1, to take a three games to one lead.

Through all of this, Grant Fuhr, The Rock, never changed. Win or lose, he was the same. The next day he played thirty-six holes of golf. "How could you possibly play thirty-six holes in the middle of the Stanley Cup finals?" a reporter asked him.

"Because," said Grant, "there wasn't time to play fifty-four."

Now all we needed was Game Five and the title was ours. That's when it came out in the papers that our mayor and the city had planned a giant parade and reception for us for the day after Game Five. Terrific. The one thing a professional athlete hates most is to be embarrassed. Imagine the Flyers' surprise on picking up the paper that morning and reading that they were supposed to be a sure-thing loss.

I knew it was going to be the kiss of death and that the Flyers would rain on our parade, and they did, 4–3. That sent us back to the City of Brotherly Bruises for Game Six, which we lost. What lay ahead of us three days later in Edmonton was Game Seven — the first Game Seven in a Stanley Cup final in sixteen years.

Then we caught *them* with their manners down and had a little fun. It turned out the Flyers had been taking the Cup into their locker room before games. I guess they were doing it for good luck and inspiration — sort of like The Door — but it wasn't right. What were they doing with it? Etching their names into it? Practicing sipping out of it? We thought it was uncool, so our trainer, Sparky, stole it from them and hid it under one of the benches in his trainer's room. Here was this historic game coming up, and five minutes before faceoff, the league couldn't find the Stanley Cup. You should have seen the bigwigs from the NHL panic. Sparky finally gave it back to them about three minutes before faceoff.

We were as jacked up for that game as for any in our lives. Guys were pacing around yelling, "This is the game you dream about playing YOUR WHOLE LIFE!" Guys had eyes as big as dinner plates. The feeling was everywhere. By game time, we knew we were going to win it. We could have played that game twenty times and won it twenty times.

Philly scored first on a five-on-three and we didn't care. We knew it was our game. Glennie and Mark's line got the goal right back. Then Tik dug the puck out of the corner and got it to me and I did what I do best — passed it to Jari. We led 2–1. From then on, we were all over them. They got two shots, total. Glennie found one more hole in Hextall's glove and it was all over but . . . the parade.

Winning that Cup changed our place in hockey history. By winning it back, we had not only cleared our name of the drug charges, but of the choke charges, too. We proved ourselves champions. The future looked great again.

. Walter and Phyllis before
was born. Everything I am
oday, and everything I
ave today, I owe to them.

. Cute as a button. What
lse can I say? I keep this
icture around to show
anet when she says Paulina
ooks just like her. I think
he looks exactly like me!

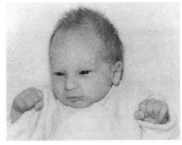

. You can see the grass coming up behind the "Wally Coliseum."
Somehow, he kept it firm and ready for us to use, even in spring. I
never knew how. It was magic.

4-5. We were really close to our grandparents. Mary and Tony were important to us in every way. Here's Kim, Tony, Keith and me.

6. It was a kick driving the tractor in my grandmother's garden.

7. I didn't realize how small I was until I saw this picture.
I was six years old. Most of the other guys were eleven.

8. My first goal. My *only* goal that first season.

9. This first year was the only year I had no pressure as a player. I loved it! I didn't even expect to make the team. It was a gift.

10. Ace Bailey was my best friend, my teacher.

11. This is my eighteenth birthday cake before my teammates sat on it. That's Ace Bailey on my left.

12. Playing with Gordie Howe is a dream come true for anybody. He was far and away my favorite player.

13. Tying Phil Esposito's record in Detroit.

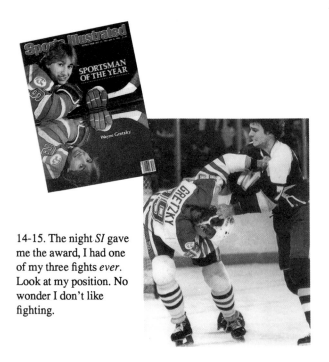

14-15. The night *SI* gave me the award, I had one of my three fights *ever*. Look at my position. No wonder I don't like fighting.

16. Kevin Lowe, one of my best friends in the world.

17. Andy Moog, a truly underrated goalie. He has made a real difference in the league.

18. 1983 was pretty grim. A whole year of hard work down the drain.

19. Joey kept everything in perspective for us. He didn't just pick up towels, he picked up spirits.

20. Grant Fuhr was the best goaltender who ever lived. If I had to play one game for everything I owned I'd pick Grant to be my goalie.

21. OK, so maybe I wasn't the best big brother in the world, but how many big brothers can give you a ride like this?

22. This is still my favorite Cup. The first one is always the best. The whole city won with us. We knew a lot of the people in the seats personally and quite a few of them got to drink out of the Cup with us.

23. I was happier for Mess winning the Conn Smythe than any trophy I ever won.

24. Mess and me. My other best friend in the whole world.

25. Paul Coffey and I had a special relationship. I was more comfortable being myself around him than with just about anybody.

26. The last Cup. I asked for a group photo, which I'd never done before. It was instinct. Janet and Walter already knew the bad news, but thankfully waited until after the celebration to tell me.

27. I put all worries about the trade out of my mind on the day Janet I were married. It was the happiest day of my life.

28. Mike Barnett and me. Over the years we've had a lot to celebrate!

29-30. Even I didn't know how much news the trade was going to make. My tears were real. I knew how hard it was going to be leaving all my friends on and off the ice. I knew my life was changing radically.

31. This was taken only five hours later but it seemed like it was years later.

32-33. Game #1 at Edmonton.

34. Marty McSorley always looks over my shoulder for me.

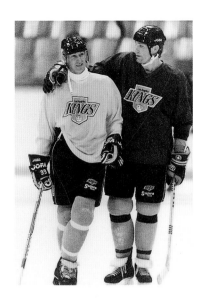

35-36. Tomas Sandstrom and Tony Granato. With these two guys playing beside me, I'm looking forward to the new seasons ahead.

37. It's all pretty exciting. This was the one record I wasn't looking forward to breaking. No one will ever take Gordie's place. But it was either break the biggest record in hockey, or stop breathing.

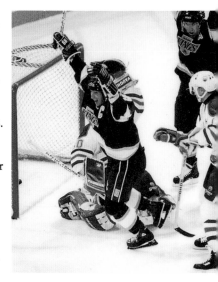

38. I always felt Gordie and I were linked in some way by Fate. Janet and Walter knew how much this moment meant to me.

9. Paulina Mary Jean Gretzky. She has taught me all about the
wonders of being a dad.

40. This shows how much I love playing in L.A. I miss Edmonton. But I love my new teammates.

41. Janet with our son, Ty Robert.

10

How to Get Married Twice in One Day

The greatest game of my life might not have been a hockey game. It might have been a Celtics-Lakers game. I was there with Alan Thicke, the TV star, and Bruce McNall, the L.A. Kings owner. Before the game CBS wanted to interview me and I said no thanks, I think I'll just watch the game. But they kept asking, so I finally said OK. You know, if I wasn't such a wimp with the press, I might still be single today.

The lights from the TV camera caused a girl sitting two sections away to look over and see who was getting interviewed. When she saw it was me, she decided to stop over and say hi. I'm glad she did. It changed my life. It was Janet Jones.

I first met Janet in 1981, the same year I made

my memorable silver screen acting debut on "The Young and the Restless." That year I was a celebrity judge on "Dance Fever," the dance contest show. I was a judge with a guy from "Magnum P.I." and Zsa Zsa Gabor. One of the dancers was a sixteen-year-old from St. Louis named Janet Jones. She was gorgeous, with legs up to here, beautiful face, blond hair and lots of curves where girls are supposed to have curves. I must have made a big impression on her, too. To this day, she doesn't have the vaguest memory of me being on that show.

But for the next six years, we kept running into each other under the weirdest circumstances. Just one more example of my dad's destiny thing. I rented a condo in Malibu that next summer and it turned out the condo next door was owned by the Van Patten family. Vince Van Patten, the tennis player and actor, happened to be the brother of Nels Van Patten, Janet's boyfriend. When she and I saw each other there was no big spark. We just said hello.

Months later, Nels invited me to his celebrity tennis tournament and Janet was there again and we all hung around, but again, there was no big spark. She had her career and her life and I had mine.

Her career, of course, was going bonkers. Like me, she'd been sort of a teenage prodigy. She'd won the Miss Dance America contest at sixteen and moved to Hollywood not long after. Like me, she was years younger than anybody else around her and had to learn to cope with success. Her first movie, *The Flamingo Kid*, was a smash hit and she had gotten great reviews. She played Matt Dillon's girlfriend. Janet became instantly famous for that role, especially for the way she looked in that drop-dead white swimsuit. Whenever people mention Janet Jones, the first thing they say is, "Oh, yeah, the girl in the white swimsuit." What people don't know about that swimsuit is that the producers wanted her to wear a real old, red, ugly, 1963 June Cleaver swimsuit, but Janet begged them to let her wear something else. She went out and bought the white swimsuit that day.

Then she starred opposite Mitch Gaylord in *American Anthem* and she had a big part in *Police Academy IV*. She was also dancing and modeling and doing *Life* covers and everything else under the sun.

A year after the tennis tournament, we bumped into each other again, out of the blue, in New York at one of my favorite New York restaurants, Il Vagabondo. She was with Nels. No sparks. Twice more in New York and once more in Los Angeles we ran into each other. Fine. We didn't see each other for three years after that. But then came the Lakers-Celtics game in 1987. As soon as I saw her again, it seemed a little different. We'd each broken up recently and now there was suddenly something there. I invited her to have a beer with us after the game in the Forum Club and she came this close to not coming. For one thing, she hates beer. (I tease her now: "You *really* must have liked me because you don't even drink. And you had TWO beers that night!") For another thing, she'd promised somebody else to have a drink with them. But she showed up and we started talking and we felt comfortable and then it slipped out that both of us were free again. Hello, sparks.

How do you know you're in love? She knew it that night and I knew it that night. It's not so much a churning in your stomach as it is the feeling that you can trust this person one hundred percent, that you could hang around with this person all day and half the night and the next three days and nights and still be laughing and talking. After the beers, we kept it going. We went out to dinner with Alan and a friend to a place in Studio City called La Serre and we had a great time. I asked for her phone number.

It just so happened that we were going to be in Toronto at the same time, so we got together there about a month later. We just walked around, went to some cafés, talked. She had spent her childhood dancing. She'd walk home from the dance studio rather then leave early when she had a ride. Just like me at the rink. Our high school lives were alike. Neither one of us went to a prom. In fact, both of us were so deep into our careers by our senior years that neither of us actually got our diploma. She's one class away, too. We both traveled all the time, yet we both hated to travel. We were still so young, yet we'd seen so much. We both loved kids and big families and we both wanted that next in our lives. We commiserated with each other and laughed and plotted. We were kind of leaning on each other's shoulders and it felt terrific. Any fool could see we were in love.

We kept making up excuses to be together. We

spent a couple of weeks in L.A. together and then another at Paul Coffey's cottage in the beautiful wilderness area of northern Ontario. Right after that, I was supposed to go to the Wimbledon tennis tournament in London. You've got to understand, all my life I'd wanted to go to Wimbledon and every time I've tried, something has messed it up. Wimbledon is my life's dream. That year, I was determined to go . . .

"What are you going to do next?" I asked her.

"I've got to go back to L.A."

"Great, I'll come, too."

I turned in my Wimbledon tickets without a second thought. Maybe next year. By now it was late August and I had to go to training camp for the 1987 Canada Cup. It was put-up-or-shut-up time. We knew then that if she came everybody was going to find out. This time she didn't hesitate. She came. The first photographer who snapped our picture sort of pulled the camera away from his face, looked at us again as if to check if what he *thought* he'd seen through his viewfinder was really there, and then made like an Olympic sprinter to his newspaper.

Janet had never seen a hockey game in her life. In fact, the first game she saw was a preliminary game against the Soviets. I said to her, "We're going to get beat about 9–1." She figured I was just trying to be humble, but I knew it was true. We weren't ready yet. We went out and got beat 10–1. After the game, she looked at me like I was an alien or something. "How did you *know* that?" she said. The other thing she couldn't figure out was why I wasn't on the ice all the time. Every forty seconds, I took a rest. "Are you feeling OK?"

Naturally, once our relationship went public, people felt compelled to give me flak. Some were offended that I'd fallen in love with an American and not a Canadian. That's so stupid I don't even want to talk about it. Others were upset that I was going out with a *Playboy* magazine centerfold. Janet had done a photo layout for *Playboy* that ran in the March 1987 issue, but it wasn't the center-fold. In fact, there was no nudity at all. *Vogue* shows twice as much as *Playboy* showed of Janet.

I thought it was stupid that so many Canadians saw a relationship between the *Playboy* pictures and Janet being an American. Canadian girls are constantly in the *Playboy* centerfold. Kimberly Conrad, who ended up marrying Hugh Hefner, is Canadian and so were Shannon Tweed and Dorothy Stratten. And they weren't just center-folds, they were Playmates of the Year. Yet here were all these Canadian holier-than-thou types telling me, "How could you date a centerfold? "

It didn't matter. You could've called her any-thing and I still would've wanted to see her. In fact, from September until January, I tried to see her as much as Air Canada would allow. I was totally, hopelessly in love with her. Still am.

I love the fact that she was a total tomboy as a kid. She was an all-star softball player who turned her cleats in for pink tights. She's nuts about sports and loves to compete. We practically kill each other on the tennis court. We kid like best friends, too. She gets us into these involved, crazy, matchmaking messes that you only see on *I Love Lucy* so sometimes I call her Lucy. And whenever I screw something up or do something dumb, she calls me Dwayne, as in, "Nice going, Dwwwwwwwayne."

I love how we talk. We can go to a movie and come out and talk about it for an hour. In those first few months, it didn't matter who was around us, we couldn't stop talking to each other.

I love how kind she is. She's the kindest person I've ever known. One of the first times she met my Aunt Ellen, the one with Down syndrome, she took her out for a manicure and a pedicure. Of course, Aunt Ellen had never had either one in her life. Nobody had ever done that for her. Nobody had ever *thought* to do that for her. Aunt Ellen didn't stop talking about that for two months.

I love how emotional Janet is. She'll cry at a Kodak ad. She was watching George Steinbrenner on TV one night talking about the death of Bart Giamatti and she started crying. And she didn't know either of them. She's very emotional about that kind of stuff. She lost her father to lung cancer when she was seventeen and now every time she visits my dad, she tries to hide his cigarettes. She's serious. She'll give him a big hug and look him in the eye and say, "Wally, Paulina needs a grandfather."

Anyway, it became clear to me that I had to have this woman in my life. She seemed to feel the same. Kids and a home and a family were so important to her that she was willing to move to Edmonton and give up her career. Amazing. We're talking about one of the hottest careers in Hollywood and she was willing to just punt it. I loved her for that.

In January, I went out and bought a diamond ring, even though I knew I wasn't going to see her for weeks. She had to go to South Carolina to film a video workout tape. I had hurt my knee and I missed her and I was just miserable. It was the day after her twenty-seventh birthday and I just couldn't wait anymore. I called her up and we got around to talking about, as usual, kids, and how many kids we wanted. Finally, I said, "Don't you want to be married before we have kids?"

"Yeah," she said.

"Well," I stammered. "This is crazy. Let's just get married."

"Is that a proposal?"

"Yeah, I think it is. Wanna get married?"

"Yeah!"

And that was it. No moonlight canoe rides or proposals in lights on a stadium scoreboard or anything. It was engagement via Bell Canada. She said yes and I was about to bust. I told some friend at dinner that night, celebrated with a few Drambuies, then went to Mark Messier's apartment, woke him up at 4:00 in the morning and announced, "MESS! I'M GETTIN' MARRIED!"

At 7:00, there was a pounding on my door. I had unplugged the phone (you know how many idiots call people in the middle of the night). I staggered out of bed to find Mike Barnett looking frantic in my hallway. "Your dad and mom have been trying to call you for two hours. They don't know what to tell the press. Why didn't you tell them you got engaged?"

The story was out. Apparently, the bartender at the restaurant that night had overheard me telling my friend and called it into the local radio station. That station was paying $1000 to the person who gave them the hottest scoop of the month and the bartender must have needed the $1000.

Janet and I decided to get married in Edmonton, since that was going to be our home. The wedding was scheduled for July 16, seven months from then. Many was the day we regretted the decision to marry in Edmonton. It got crazy. Even the tiniest, most remote fact made front-page headlines. Also nonfacts, especially about costs.

JANET'S DRESS TO COST $40,000

CHAMPAGNE TO BE $3000 PER BOTTLE

JANET'S RING: $100,000

None of it was true. It got so bad I had to hold a press conference. Can you imagine having to call a press conference about your own wedding? I had to set the record straight. Edmonton's economy was real down, because of oil prices, and I wasn't going to let people think I was squandering $1 million on a wedding. The champagne was free, a friend of mine donated it. The wedding dress wasn't near $40,000. It had forty thousand sequins. The ring wasn't cheap, but nothing like *that*. Hey, even the beer was free. Neither Molson nor Labatts would let the other one donate the beer, so I had to let both of them do it.

But it wasn't just the press. It was the constant questions, like "Why aren't you getting married in the Coliseum?" One night Janet said to me, "Let's elope." And we almost did. We went to dinner and talked all night about it. Finally we decided we couldn't do it to our parents.

So the wedding was held as scheduled. The papers were calling it "Canada's Royal Wedding," and I can't imagine what a bigger one would be like. How many weddings have you been to with two hundred credentialed media, network coverage, massive security, the Edmonton fire department lining the steps to the cathedral adorned in their dress reds, 700 guests, ten thousand people waiting outside the church to get a glimpse of the wedding party, a twenty-foot detachable train on the wedding dress and a death threat?

Sure. What's a Gretzky event without a death threat? The morning of the wedding, the chief inspector of the RCMP told my dad and I that somebody had walked into a 7-11 store and left a note that said, "St. Jasper's is going up in smoke." The police checked it out and told us, "Our recommendation is to proceed." We took a gulp and said, "OK."

Still, when Janet's brother John brought Janet up the aisle, it all became worth it. I guess I'd forgotten what was going to happen or what we were actually doing, but that was one of the most stunning moments of my life. When I looked back and saw this beautiful woman, really radiant, really incredible, I think I went flush red. But more than just how she looked, I realized that I was marrying someone I could spend this lifetime with and about nine others past that.

From then on, I was on a total high. Halfway through the vows, the preacher asked me to say,

"Janet, I take you to be my wife." So I said, "Janet, I take you to be my wife." But he kind of got lost in his book or something and I thought he didn't hear me or that I was supposed to say something, so I said it again. "Janet, I take you to be my wife." Hey, there were 700 people in that church and I was more nervous than in any Game Seven I've ever played in. Nobody else caught it, but Janet did. She was biting on her lip, trying not to break out laughing right there at the altar. But so what? The way I look at it, we're married double.

One of the best parts was that both my grandmothers got to be there. My father's mother was sick, but she had seemed to improve a little for the wedding. And as soon as it was over, we told her what hardly anybody knew: Janet was four and a half months pregnant. She'd gotten pregnant at the end of March, a month and a half after our engagement. Take a look at any picture of her in that wedding dress and you can't tell. But she was. It's like I tell people, I gave her a cream and tan Rolls-Royce Corniche for a wedding present, but it was nothing compared to what she gave me: Paulina.

The reception was a gas. Alan Thicke was master of ceremonies. My best man, Eddie Mio, got up and said, "Uh, folks, Wayne has asked me to do him a favor. When he first came to Edmonton, he knew he was going to be meeting a lot of girls, so he had thirty keys to his apartment made up. During his single days, he ended up giving them all out. Now he's asked me to try to get all those keys back. So, please, all the girls here who have a key kindly bring them up to the podium now and put them in this basket."

So, one by one, all these supposed ex-girlfriends of mine came up and put keys in the basket. Toward about number twenty-seven or twenty-eight, it started getting hilarious. Paul Coffey's mom came up with one. Then came Dalyce Barnett, Mike's wife, who was seven months pregnant.

"OK, but that's only twenty-nine," Eddie said. "We're missing one key. Come on, who has it?"

Slowly, the last person rose, sort of sheepishly, walked toward the podium and put it in the basket.

Gordie Howe.

11

The Last Cold War

After winning our third Stanley Cup in 1987, I didn't feel much like wearing lampshades on my head. I was beat. Oh, I sprayed beer and lived it up for a while, but when everybody was off the ice and out of the stands, I sat there on the bench with my parents. "I've never been so physically and mentally exhausted in my life," I told them. "I've had enough."

I really wanted to quit. I'd been busting my butt playing high-pressure one hundred-percent hockey since I was six years old, every year playing all the exhibition games, all the regular season games and, for four out of the last five years, every postseason game. Not to mention all the All-Star games, the Rendez-Vous games that had NHL all-stars playing the Soviets and the Canada Cups. In sixty-three days there was another Canada Cup staring me in the face, and nothing sounded worse. I was spent, my muscles felt like rubber and I was twenty-five going on fifty-five.

"Aw," said my dad, "you'll feel better after the summer."

"Nope," I said. "I think this is it for me."

The fight back from the *SI* drug story, contract problems between me and Slats and the upset loss to Calgary had taken a lot out of me. So did the constant expectations. One reporter asked me if I thought I was "past my prime," at a point in the season when I was seventy-five points ahead of the next guy.

My contract was frazzling me, too. Nobody knew it, but that entire 1986–87 season we were negotiating. It was constantly bugging me. It got so bad that at one point Peter Pocklington's lawyer threatened to sue me for $50 million if I didn't sign in the next forty-eight hours. To his credit, Pocklington told the guy to calm down. That contract was the most screwed up in history. Nobody could tell whether I was a free agent or not. The NHL even set up a five-man committee to figure it out. I finally signed a contract that we all knew was so messed up we were going to have to renegotiate it within two years. Little did I know how important that was going to be.

Anyway, I was a wet noodle. I was seriously thinking about getting out of hockey. And if I wasn't going to retire, I for sure didn't want to go through three weeks of Canada Cup training camp and then two weeks of the Cup itself. My body was screaming for a beach.

I knew the Canada Cup itself was going to be a bear. The Soviets were going to bring their best team yet and I just felt too sapped to give my best. You play these games for the honor and glory of your country and I didn't want to let Canada down.

It became a big stink all across the country. I was two months late in deciding. Finally, my dad put it to me flat out. "If you don't play, you're going to take all kinds of heat," he said. "If you *do* play, but play badly, you'll take even more heat. Your only choice is to play and play well." As usual, he was right. I said yes, probably because I imagined myself watching the Canada Cup instead of playing in it and it felt lousy.

Looking back on it, it was probably the best hockey decision I ever made, even though it didn't look that way at first.

We had played the first game of the series at 6:00 P.M. against Czechoslovakia on a Saturday night and we had Sunday off, so after dinner some of the guys wanted to go out for a beer. We found out that was forbidden. Mike Keenan, the head coach, nearly had a mutiny on his hands. A lot of the players were furious, so Bobby Clarke asked some of us to go to Mike and get it cleared up. Basically, the problem came down to Mike not believing we were dedicated to the cause.

Keenan: "All I want to know is, do you care about your country or not?"

Us: "Are you serious?"

Keenan: "OK, there'll never be a problem again."

And there wasn't.

That was a great team we put together. There was Mess, Cof, Anderson, Grant, me, Mario Lemieux, Dale Hawerchuk, Ray Bourque, Brent Sutter, Larry Murphy, all kinds of great players. That team was so terrific we actually *cut* Steve Yzerman, who'd 102 points that year. I was glad to see Hawerchuk on my side for once. He was one of three guys in my life who hit me so hard I was knocked unconscious. I know Hawerchuk gets 100-something points a year, but I still think he's the most underrated guy in the league. When the pressure is on, he always comes through. His only problem is that until recently he's been with a team, Winnipeg, that can't quite get off the ground, so mostly he's gone unnoticed. The world needs to discover this guy, and now that he's in Buffalo, it'll happen.

Still, it became obvious that Dale wasn't going to be one of the big scorers on the team. He'd have to change his role. So we asked him to become a checker. He could've whined and called his agent and gone home, but he didn't. Instead, he was terrific. That's what makes the Canada Cup so fascinating. A superstar goal scorer turns into Joe Defense overnight for love of country.

And then there was Super Mario, age twenty-one. He'd already had a fifty-goal season the year before, and the year before that he'd gone crazy with 141 points. People would end up saying that I got him to bloom that Canada Cup, that I *taught* him how to score, but that's ridiculous. He was already on his way. It was just a matter of time before Mario became one of the great players in history.

If people saw a different Mario in that series, it might have been because he was inspired by playing with the rest of us. I think he was surprised how hard the Oilers practiced. He said something nice when it was all over with: "Every shift, Wayne tried to do the impossible." He learned that from Mess, too. After all, Mario was the best player on the worst team in the league, Pittsburgh. He hadn't really been around guys who *knew* how to win, who'd done it.

It's funny, people love to dream up feuds. But Mario and I hit it off during that month. We found out we weren't just friends, we were icemates. We understood each other. We went to the same holes. He likes to shoot the puck and I like to pass it. I told him one day, "On two-on-ones, give me the puck and you take the shots." I wanted him shooting, because he's got those awesome wrists. He could snap a puck through a refrigerator door. The guy stands 6'4" but he's got the touch of a 5'6" guy.

The only problem was, Keenan wasn't playing us on the same line. He was mixing us up, I guess to mix the Soviets up. In one game against the Czechs he used something like eighteen different lines. Lemieux and I finally managed to get on the same line one time and we beat Team USA 3–2 with Mario getting a hat trick. After the game, a Finnish reporter stood up at the press conference and asked: "Why not Gretzky and Lemieux, same line, all time?"

Keenan stared at him for a second and then said,

"It would be counterproductive." But a few days later Keenan said, "I've changed my mind." Lemieux and I would play on "same line, all time" from then on. Having both of us on the same shift really messed the Soviets up. Of the four goals Mario scored in the final with the Soviets, I assisted on all four of them.

We knew the Soviets had a great team. I mean, a *great* team. My old friend Tretiak was gone, but they were still loaded. Their defenseman, Viacheslav Fetisov, was fantastic and so was their great center, Igor Larionov, both of whom ended up in the NHL. Makarov made it to the NHL, too, and they're all making big money now in North America. Meanwhile, Tretiak, the greatest Soviet player of all, never made a dime.

He'd always ask me how much money he could make in the NHL. I'd say, "It depends. If you played for the New York Rangers, you'd probably make $800,000 a year. If you played in St Louis, you might only make $300,000."

He was baffled by that.

"If I play same?"

"Right."

"I make so much more in one city and so much less in other city, even though I same man?"

"You got it."

Some people were surprised that the Soviets who joined the NHL had a hard time of it, but I wasn't. The biggest adjustment for those guys was going to be off the ice, not on it. Come to think of it, if you shipped me off to Moscow, I'd probably be miserable — and play awful — too. I knew Larionov would do well, though, because he speaks better English than a lot of North Americans. And I think that's why he had the good year. He's also given the NHL more than just his skating. For one thing, he's told the truth. He told how the KGB would have fresh urine supplies waiting for them whenever they went through drug testing in international hockey events. He's also one of the most caring men I've ever known. When he heard there was an AIDS epidemic in his hometown in the Soviet Union, he bought ten thousand syringes as a Christmas present for the hospital there. Apparently a dozen people were catching AIDS from using one dirty needle.

But besides Igor, no other Soviet did much. I think the Soviet way of hockey has lost a lot of its dominance. Canada is the far better hockey country now. That's not how it used to be. The Russian philosophy was the right one — give the kids a puck and let them have fun. That's how the Soviet players developed such great skills. The Canadian philosophy was make them skate first, then you throw them the puck. But so many Canadian coaches learned how the Soviets play through watching the Canada Cup and other international competitions that we've now adopted their system. We've learned from the Soviets how to handle the puck, how to be creative on offense. Our current top twenty now are better than the Soviet top twenty. And if you took the two hundred best NHL players and the two hundred best Soviets, the Canadians would dominate the Soviet league. Look at the World Championships now. Canada has killed them lately. Overall, we've learned more from them than they've learned from us.

Canada will still have trouble in the 1992 Olympics and might lose to the Soviets, but it's only because we send such a young team over there compared to the Soviet team. If they ever change the rules and allow the NHL players, of course, it would be a totally different story. By the way, I'd sign up in two seconds.

Anyway, the way we look at the Soviet players now is a whole lot different than we looked at them going into that Canada Cup: evil, silent, coldblooded killers out to take a cup with *our* name on it. They mauled us in the preliminary games. But the more we practiced, the better we got. We tied them in the first game of the round-robin tournament, 3–3, and then beat them 5–2 in the last tune-up. You could just tell this was going to be a great series.

We played Game One of the finals in Montreal, got down 4–1 but came back and eventually went ahead 5–4 on my goal with three minutes left. Somebody shot it off the boards and I picked up the rebound and banged it off the goalie and in. But then I let them tie it up. I stayed on a shift too long and got tired. I just missed my chance to get off. The play went behind our end, and Andrei Khomutov, my man, went around me, threw it in front of the net and it bounced off Ray Bourque's skate for the tying goal. Then the Soviets' Alexander Semak jammed it high in overtime to win it. In a best-of-three series, we were down 1–0. After the game, the first thing my dad said to me was, "You were on the ice too long for that fifth goal." I hate it when he's right.

Two days later, as I was making my way to Copps Coliseum in Hamilton, Ontario, for Game Two, I had no idea that I was about to play in the greatest hockey game ever, or that I was going to play the greatest game *I'd* ever played. Put it this way: my average ice time in a game is about twenty-four minutes. That night I played fifty. I was double- and triple-shifting. Messier and Lemieux were also on the ice a lot. It was grueling. I was as exhausted as I've ever been after any game, bar none.

It was nose to nose the whole night. Neither team would let the other get up by more than two goals. We let a 3–1 first period lead get tied 4–4 in the third. I was playing my butt off and doing everything as well as I could do it. Maybe I was making up for my Game One defensive screwup. By the time it was 4–4, I had three assists, the last one to Lemieux.

With ten minutes left, we got a power play goal from Mario off my pass to make it 5–4. We held them off for the next eight minutes and we figured we had the game. But then with just a little under two minutes to go, Valeri Kamensky tied it up with an unbelievable shot, a chop shot over Grant's shoulder as Kamensky was falling down. As we dragged ourselves to the locker room, we could hardly believe it. Overtime.

That first overtime was so exhausting, I literally could not control my muscles. I had given everything I had in my body and there was nothing left. I mean this hockey game was up and down, no clutching or grabbing, just nonstop skating. And as I was sitting there on the bench, totally spent, something unexpected happened. Unexpected and embarrassing.

I peed in my pants.

I was so completely exhausted that I had no control of those muscles. I couldn't stop it. There was nothing I could do. It was like marathon runners get toward the twenty-sixth mile, when they don't have the strength to control it.

All of a sudden someone was saying, "Gretz, you're up."

Nobody knew, but after the game, I told everybody. They laughed for a half hour.

Amazingly, nobody scored in that overtime and we had to go through *another*. If I could barely make it through one overtime, what would my body be like in two? But halfway through it, Larry Murphy, a defenseman, took a shot that bounced off the post to me. I was trying to shoot it in, but when I swung at it, it sort of squirted off my stick right to Mario, who just punched it in and we won. To this day, everybody thinks it was the greatest pass in the world — my fifth assist of the night — but it was luck, pure and simple. Keep it quiet, though, would you?

I think I lay on the ice for about ten minutes. If somebody had handed me a pillow and a blanket, I'd have slept right there. That was the craziest night. It felt like we'd been in a war. The game ended at 12:45 in the morning. By the time we left the locker room it was almost 2:00. And yet people had newspapers with the score and the story of the game in it. It was unreal.

Since we were so close to home, Janet and I drove the twenty minutes the next day to Brantford to see my folks. Remember, these were the first hockey games my wife had ever seen and she was loving it. "Boy, this is the *greatest* stuff I've ever watched. I love hockey! I can't wait until the NHL season starts!"

What could I tell her? It's like this every night?

We all knew Game Three was going to be a huge game. They were going to check Mess like crazy and Mario worse and me just as bad. I was already so sore that I was getting two massages a day. I remember telling the masseuse, "We need some big goals tonight or we can't win."

So what do we do? We go out and get some big nothings. The Soviets got up 3–0 on us before we even got untracked. We were all thinking the same awful thought: here comes 8–1 in '81 again. But then the Flyers' Rick Tocchet got a goal for us and Murphy, Brent Sutter and Dale got goals and all of a sudden we were ahead, 5–4. We were playing as hard as we could, but the Soviets wouldn't be denied. With eight minutes to go, Semak nailed us again to make it 5–5.

I'm thinking, "My body will NOT make another overtime." I was serious. I thought if I went another overtime, I might throw up. There were two minutes left in regulation time. We had a faceoff in our own end. That's when Keenan did something most people felt was strange. He sent me out to the faceoff circle, but had Dale step in at the last second and take it. Coffey and Murphy and Mario were out there, too. We had all our big scorers on the ice. It was a big gamble, since Mess is our best faceoff man.

Right away I noticed something. For the first time in the finals, the guy who had been blanketing me, Fetisov, wasn't in my face. He wasn't even on the ice. Instead it was a twenty-one-year-old kid, Igor Kravchuk. To this day, I still don't know why they did that.

Somehow, Hawerchuk won the faceoff from Valeri Kamensky — the biggest faceoff of his life — Mario tipped the puck out and I snapped it up at the blue line. Hawerchuk had checked Mario's man and all of a sudden we were on a three-on-one, with Kravchuk in front of me, Mario trailing me to my left and Murphy to my right.

Now Larry Murphy is a nice guy and a good player, but there's no way in a thousand years he was going to get that puck. He knew it, too, so he made a brilliant move. He went straight to the net. I kept faking to pass to him and Kravchuk had no choice but to go with him. That's when I threw it gently back to Mario, who was all alone.

Mario wound up that howitzer of his and blistered it into the Soviet net. I jumped about five feet into the air and into his arms. I was so tired I could barely hold on. We crashed to the ice and I screamed in his ear, "Mario, don't move!" I was utterly exhausted and so was he. There was one minute and twenty-six seconds left. I wanted to just stay right there and savor the feeling. The fans were going nuts. Our teammates were jumping all around us. It was a great moment, an unforgettable moment. We held them off the rest of the way and it was over. No more overtimes. Vacation.

Winning the Stanley Cup is a sweet, sweet feeling, and when you win it, you don't believe anything can match it. But winning that Canada Cup is every bit as sweet in a different way. We get paid millions of dollars to do our best for the NHL, but we play the Canada Cup for our country and for our players' association and for the love of the game. And when you do it for those reasons, and you play the hardest and best hockey of your life, the payoff seems pure and lasting and unforgettable.

That series was the end of the Soviet-Canada hockey wars. Two years later, the Soviets allowed their stars to join the NHL. The mystique of defeating the Soviets is now gone. Oh, we'll play them again, but look around. The Berlin Wall is down, the domination of the Communist Party is history, the Soviets are moving toward freedom of speech and freedom of the press. It's a far better world now than it was just a year or two ago. And because of it the Canada Cup will never be the same.

I can live with that.

12

Crumbling Walls

I respect Glen Sather, and think he's one of the best hockey minds I've ever been around, but our relationship was starting to get touchy about this time.

All our winning and success hadn't mellowed him at all. If anything, it was like none of it had happened. To him, we hadn't proven a thing. He didn't think I should have limits. If I scored four goals, he'd be on my butt for not getting five. I guess that was just Slats's way of motivating people, but it's too bad he never learned that type of thing never motivated me. Everybody's different.

His style wasn't going over so big with Jari or Coffey, either. In fact, Sather was the one who drove Cof out of Edmonton. Slats used to yell at Coffey on the bench: "You're not into it! You refuse to play defense!" And he'd bash him publicly, too. "It would be interesting to see if Paul could play the same way the rest of the year that he plays in October and November," Slats said one day in the papers.

He was calling Coffey lazy. That drove Paul out of his mind. He bashed Slats right back in the papers. "If he starts pointing fingers," Cof said. "That sucks. It's pretty shallow. I'm sick of it. Seven years, it's been the same thing, game in and game out. We should be treated a little better. We don't need to be treated like this."

That those problems got into the papers only made matters worse. It was the beginning of the end. The end itself probably came in a game against Vancouver toward the end of the year. Sather didn't play him at the end of the game even though Paul only needed one point to break Bobby Orr's points record for a defenseman. Paul was hurt. Let's face it, we were playing a nineteenth-place hockey team. Don't you think we'd have been as safe with Paul Coffey out there as anybody else? I always wondered if that was just Slats's way of humbling Paul a little, or simply Slats's usual procedure of putting the team ahead of any individual.

I'm not sure Cof ever respected Slats after that. I remember one day, Paul and I were at practice and we looked down and saw Slats teaching guys slap shot techniques. I said just kiddingly, "Here's a guy teaching people how to score goals, and he got 90 his whole career!" But Paul didn't stop laughing for a week.

In the end, Paul's pride had been wounded too badly. Edmonton ended up offering more money than Pittsburgh, but Paul was never coming back to play for the Oilers. He went to Pittsburgh.

Slats's "motivation techniques" even got to the unflappable one, Grant Fuhr. The year after I left, I heard about Slats and Grant trading barbs in the Edmonton papers. Grant got so fed up with Slats referring to him being out of shape that Grant quit. All that he has ever wanted in hockey was to play well, have fun and be respected. Now he was having no fun. Somehow, Slats talked him back into playing.

Despite all the damage it created, I'm convinced Slats didn't mean anything personal in it. It was just Slats's ethic. He was a scrappy little player during the ten years he played in the league for six different teams. He never had an abundance of talent, so he learned to do anything it took to win. He loved winning more than anything. It killed him to lose. If he lost one game, it was like the end of the world. He'd get all red and slam his door and stew and fret about it.

Every once in a while, he could make fun of himself, though. One night in New York I was feeling lousy. My knee was killing me. I'd slept all night with an ice pack on it. The trainer, Peter Millar, had to call me every hour to wake me up so I'd straighten it out. When I tried to skate in the morning, I couldn't. I told Slats, "I think I'm out."

"Nooooo," Slats said. Then he ran to the training room, came back with two aspirins and taped them to my knee. I laughed and said I'd give it a try. I got three goals that night.

I'll admit it, Slats could be a great motivator. To get us jacked up to play the Islanders in the playoffs in my second year, he rolled in a television set just minutes before faceoff. It was a video he'd put together of us whipping the Canadiens while Tom Jones sang "The Impossible Dream" behind it. We had goosebumps the size of tennis balls.

Slats was unpredictable. One minute he'd be all over you for something tiny, the next minute he'd be cutting up in the locker room like a kid, keeping everybody loose, having a great time. He was famous for dousing you with ice cold water in the shower or secretly filling your hairbrush with shaving cream. His thinking was ahead of its time. He let us play the music as loud as we wanted, let Jari and me play ping-pong almost right up to faceoff, let me sit and watch the broadcast of the game between periods. He was a players' coach that way.

Then again, he could be arrogant. With me, he decided I was at a point in my career where I'd start going soft if he didn't stay on me every step of the way. And the way he did that was through the papers. Slats had a certain way with the papers. Whatever he wanted written eventually got written and what he wanted left out stayed out. If I had a bad game, he'd say, "Gretzky stunk tonight" and it would be headlines. If he said, "Gretzky's playing bad," all the fans would want to know why I was playing so bad. One day he called me "pampered." I'll never forget the time he said, "We've got to get Wayne and Kurri going." I'd just scored thirteen points in the last four games.

Janet could tell I wasn't happy. She'd see me come home sometimes after getting four or five points and honestly have tears in my eyes because of the way I was being treated. "Wayne, you don't deserve this," she'd say. And everybody else I knew began to tell me the same thing.

I guess that was Glen's management style, to put the high-scoring player down and lift the other ones up, but that doesn't make it right. I don't need to be patted on the back twenty-four hours a day, but there are times when you can go up to a guy privately and say, "Way to go. You're doing a good job." Everybody has pride. You can't get bashed every day and not be expected to feel it.

Slats wasn't too popular that year with the guys in the back of the bus, although to his credit he always built a winner. He traded the funniest guy on the team, Semenko, to Hartford. We had picked up Reijo Ruotsalainen, a Finnish defenseman, and Semenko was out. On paper, I guess it was a smart hockey deal, but it changed the feel of the team, as good as Reijo was. A hockey team isn't made up only of sticks and pucks and skates. A hockey team is a collection of people and the magic between the people has to be right. Semenko was a big part of that team for us, and not just on the ice.

Still, that was still a great team. We'd lost Cof's speed up the ice and his shot on the power play, true, but Craig Simpson had fantastic hands. We blew through the league again that year and I even got some time off — the hard way. I smashed up my knee in a game with Philadelphia and missed the next sixteen games. I got sandwiched at the net and put a little tear in the cartilage. It was the best thing that could've happened to me. Without that break, I'd have been a zombie come playoff time.

A month after I came back, I broke Gordie Howe's all-time record for assists against — who else? — the Kings. The old record was 1,049. That's an achievement I'm really proud of. I broke that record in 681 games, 1,086 games less than it took Gordie to set it. You'll never catch me bragging about goals, but I'll talk all you want about my assists. Hockey is a team game, and to me assists are the ultimate "team" stat. If you ever get a chance to see an NHL scorer's card, you'll see it says, across the top: "OFFICIAL SCORERS BE PARTICULAR TO GIVE CREDIT FOR ASSISTS." That's a rarity, an NHL policy I agree with completely.

And who else should get the goal on that record assist but Jari? They stopped the game and Mark and Kevin gave me a gold stick engraved with the name of every player I'd ever assisted on a goal. It's the nicest memento I have.

But Slats was doing his best to wipe any smiles off my face. In Buffalo one night, he benched Jari, Tik and me. "You guys aren't pulling your weight!" he screamed at us. I got on the ice for two minutes in the third period, total. I was furious.

"You can say I didn't play well tonight or I sucked tonight," I said in his office after the game, "but don't *ever* say that I don't give it my all every night! When I play, I play my hardest and you know it!"

He started to back down a little bit. "Wayne, I was just trying to motivate you. Maybe I'm a little tough on you sometimes. You stay here, I'll go talk to the press and soften it."

That really infuriated me. I was out of my mind I was so mad. It was a final blow to our relationship.

When I think back on how it all went bad with Slats and Pocklington, I think it started with money. They would always tell the press, "We're paying him $1 million," but they weren't. My base salary was a lot lower than that. The only way I'd make $1 million was by winning the MVP, the Ross, being first-team All-Star, things like that, stuff that should have been bonus money over and above the million they were always referring to. What they were saying was, "We *expect* you to be all those things." Not "*Congratulations* on being all those things." It gave me an idea how much I was appreciated.

Slats basically had a problem with money. It was really his big weakness. He could never accept why the players made the money they did. When he played, Bobby Orr was making $250,000. For him to see a fringe player making that much, it bent his brain. And because he was the general manager, that sort of thinking kept the team's salaries down. When the Islanders won all those Stanley Cups, Mike Bossy kept signing huge contracts for far more than he was worth late into his career as a reward, as a way of saying thanks for the great years. But with us, Slats and Peter didn't want to share the wealth. Maybe Peter couldn't afford to share the wealth. Our cash flow supported Peter's other ventures. I'm sure Slats was under big pressure from Pocklington to keep the salaries down.

That's why he got on me. The season before, I had not signed a contract that would guarantee I'd stay with the team, so Slats made sure the public knew whenever I messed up. That way, if I left, Slats could say, "I've been telling you, he's not that great." I saw what he was doing, but still, when he'd rip me in the papers, it would tick me off. He can do it all he wants in the locker room, but outside of it, it's nobody's business.

Life was tough enough sometimes in that city without having the press on my back. My privacy was nonexistent. Edmonton is a great city, but it's only 600,000 people and the more Janet and I became a public couple, the smaller Edmonton got. When I was younger I was usually out with the guys. Now it was usually with my wife-to-be. Toward the end, it felt like a prison with restaurants. I got paranoid about us doing anything — having a beer, going to a movie — because it would be in the paper the next day. Do you know what it's like to dread reading the morning paper? Janet took the heat all the time. They'd write about what she was wearing or how she was doing her hair, stupid things. We were being smothered to death. Fortunately the general public in Edmonton was very nice to us.

Add to that the fact that for the first time since my rookie year, I didn't win the scoring title, and for the first year ever I didn't win the MVP. Mario won them both. A few writers were saying I lost the scoring race because I was distracted by Janet, that somehow she was hurting my performance. That theory was so idiotic I couldn't believe it. If anything I was playing *better* with her. She'd made me calmer.

So let's see. Sather was on my back. Pocklington was making threats about me not resigning. The press was being hard on Janet. Mario was trying to bump me down a peg. The walls were closing in on us in Edmonton. And I was unhappy.

A perfect time for the playoffs to begin.

13

We Swept Them in Five

We opened those 1988 playoffs with our usual warm-up series, Winnipeg, then went on to the series that I knew was for the Stanley Cup — Calgary. The Flames had played us the toughest all year and they had that incredible power play — Hakan Loob, Joe Nieuwendyk and Mike Bullard.

I said after our 3–1 win in Calgary in Game One that it was the biggest ever in team history. We wanted them so bad. I even got a breakaway goal that went off Vernon's glove, off the goal post and in.

Back in Edmonton, something even bigger was going on. Janet was in our apartment, feeling kind of funny. She sent my brother Glen down to the store to get a home pregnancy test. We'd decided it was the time to try to get pregnant, since the wedding was close enough that it wouldn't show. She

sent Glen because if she'd gone to the drugstore herself you can imagine the headlines:
JANET BUYS H.P.T. — RABBIT FEARED DEAD

After the game she was on the phone to me in Calgary.

"Guess what?" she said.

"What?"

"You're going to be a father."

You had to scrape me off the ceiling. I was so pumped up they had to tie me down. I couldn't wait to get home and start listening for heartbeats. I knew I was going to play great that night.

Twice we were behind by two goals in that game, but we were like cockroaches. You couldn't kill us. Jari had been off his game, but in those playoffs he was SuperKurri. We were losing 4–3 with only a couple minutes left when he robbed the defenseman and scored to take us to overtime. Then Mess got stuck with a penalty. I thought, "Uh-oh, here we go. Overtime AND a power play." But one of their defensemen shot the puck up the glass and I jumped behind him, picked it up, and skated just inside the blue line. That's when I let it fly. I have no idea why. I never take slap shots from the blue line, but I let this one go as hard as any I've ever taken in my life. I'll never forget the sight of it flying over Vernon's shoulder. I thought it was the biggest NHL goal I'd ever scored. The Flames had become a better team than us, yet we'd just beaten them two out of two in their own building.

To me, that clinched the Stanley Cup. The Flames had no chance of winning in Edmonton, especially since their coach, Terry Crisp, decided to bench John Tonelli. I wouldn't bench John Tonelli if he'd just stolen my car. I guess he and Crisp had exchanged words, and now here was one of the best players in hockey sitting around in jeans. It was a beautiful sight for the Oilers.

We won Game Three 4–2 and Game Four 6–4 and that series was history. To celebrate, I went crazy and rented a Learjet and flew Mess and Kevin and me to Las Vegas for a couple days of R & R.

But, really, the rest of the way was a cakewalk compared to playing Calgary. We pounded Detroit four out of five, which was no great achievement. It came out that a few of the Red Wings were caught drinking and missed curfew and who knows what else before Game Five in Edmonton. Their coach, Jacques Demers, blamed them for the loss.

That left us Boston to beat for the Stanley Cup. If there was one place in the league I hated it was Boston Garden. For one thing, it's hot as a steam bath in there, especially in May. For another, the rink is too small for me to play my game. There's not enough room to move. For a third, it's where Steve Kasper played. Nobody played better defense on me than Kasper. When I got married, I half expected to see Kasper standing at the altar in a tux.

We had two objectives: (1) to not let the Bruins win more than one game. Nobody had accomplished that yet. And (2) win it on the road. I don't want this to sound ungrateful, but every Stanley Cup we'd won so far was in Edmonton, and every time we'd won it, so many fans swarmed the ice that the feeling of winning it as a *team*, the feeling of accomplishing something together, was lost. You couldn't get that moment back in the locker room, either, what with all the friends and family and TV cameras and reporters. Then you'd be off for the summer and next thing you knew everybody wants to know, "Yeah, but can you do it again?" We definitely wanted to win it for ourselves in good ol' Boston Garden.

The Bruins had an old friend in goal, Andy Moog. I felt sorry for Andy. This is a guy who should have been with us. But Slats refused to play him in the big games and Andy, like all really good goaltenders, can't live that way. Andy played out his option in 1987 and wound up in Boston.

So it was on to Boston, where I'd played many a forgettable game. Larry Bird once said, "Somebody tell Gretzky that's *my* building." I thought it was a great line.

Then came a truly strange game, Game Four. To start off with, it was very warm that day. Well, since it was May 24, it was supposed to be warm. But inside the Garden, it was an oven. The heat produced a fog on the ice. For a while, you couldn't see much. It was like, "Hey, Jari, do you have the puck?"

We were down 3–2 when Simpson got a goal to tie it. Then, click, all the power went off. Ace Bailey looked around and said, "Well, they had just enough electricity in this old barn to flip the red light on and that was it." You couldn't see a thing. The only way we got back to the locker room was by the cops escorting us with flashlights.

Apparently, a four thousand-volt switch overloaded. Someone quipped it was one Ben Franklin put in. We sat for a while until one of the kids who worked there came in and said, "Those lights aren't coming back on. I've seen it happen too many times." That convinced me. I got dressed. About fifteen minutes later, they came in and said, "It's over." We were going to fly back and replay Game Four — or Four A — in Edmonton, where we were all pretty sure we'd paid our light bill. And if you think we were disappointed about having to win another Cup in Edmonton, you should have seen how the Bruins looked. Now they had to fly clear across the continent to play in front of our fans and watch them celebrate the Cup.

In the replay we were leading 3–2 with ten seconds left in the second period when, little did I know it, I was about to get my last assist as an Oiler. As I was crossing the red line, I checked the clock. People were screaming "Shoot, shoot!" Nope. I held it. Then I cut hard right at the blue line and cocked up to shoot. "Shoot, you moron!" I held it. Then, at the last possible second, I flipped it over to Simpson in the slot and he swatted it under Andy and we led 4–2.

We won that game, 7–2, and with it the Cup. But after we'd carried that Cup around again, I did something strange. I don't know why, but I got *everybody* together on the ice for a picture. Teams in the old, old days used to do it and I'd always wanted to try it. We got everybody in it. From the trainers to the players to the coaches to the scouts to the players who weren't dressed that night, anybody who had a hand in that Cup, they were all at center ice for that picture.

I had no idea it was to be my last moment as an Oiler. What better way to end it? Destiny, my dad would say. That picture now hangs in my house and I look at it all the time. That was the most talented team I ever played on. We had speed, size, scoring, defense. We were phenomenal. And that picture means more to me because of what happened right afterward.

I've got my hands on the Cup in the picture, but it probably meant even more to a lot of guys who weren't holding it. Guys like Craig MacTavish and Simpson, who had never won one before. Guys like Kevin Lowe, who played that entire playoff season with a cast on his hand and broken ribs he hadn't told anybody about. The only way I found out about it was before Game Three against Boston. "Why is your sweater so bulgy?" I asked him. "Uh, probably from the pads," he said. "I broke a couple of ribs." Looking at him, I remembered the Islanders' locker room that first final we played. So *that's* what it takes to win Stanley Cups.

I see Steve Smith in that picture. I won the Conn Smythe trophy as MVP of the playoffs that season, but I wish they'd given it to Steve, the kid who got blamed for the 1986 playoff loss. Nobody on the ice was better during those playoffs than Steve Smith.

I guess it meant a lot to Peter Pocklington, too. On the ice that night, he told me he loved me. What I didn't know was that maybe he loved me because I hadn't gotten injured, which would've messed up his plans for me.

We were a little like the Green Bay Packers: a small city that people said shouldn't ever have its own team, a close-knit bunch of guys with a close-knit bunch of fans. It was our fourth Stanley Cup in five years. Our average age was twenty-five. That was a setup nobody could screw up.

Or so we thought.

14

The Day I Made
"Transactions"

Not two hours after we'd won the Cup, we were having a celebration dinner. The season was over, the title was ours and I was feeling elated and exhausted at the same time. My wife was there and my dad and a few friends. But somewhere between the appetizer and the salad they all dropped a bomb on me.

I was in the middle of telling my dad that Janet and I were going to see if we could buy Pat Bowlen's old house in Edmonton. Bowlen owns the Denver Broncos and he was selling and we just wanted to see . . . And that's when I saw a real weird look on my dad's face.

"What's wrong?" I said.

"Uh, Wayne," he said, "I'd forget about the house if I were you."

This didn't sound good.

"Why?"

"They're trying to deal you."

"What?"

"They're trying to trade you. I swear. I know for a fact. You don't believe me, you call Nelson Skalbania. He's already called me a couple times. I've been wanting to tell you so bad. But I didn't want to upset you during the playoffs."

I couldn't believe it, but I could tell from my dad's expression that it was true. The team wanted to trade me? The team that just two hours before I'd helped to win its fourth Stanley Cup in the last five years? The team that was still young enough to win another three or four in a row? The team I assumed I'd retire with? Amazing how fast you can lose your appetite.

How could this happen? Janet and I were looking at homes in Edmonton. She'd already had her car shipped up. She'd made friends. We were about to start Lamaze classes. It was the beginning of a whole new life for us. And now they were going to deal me?

My world was rocked. Even more amazing than that was that all these people — my dad, Janet, Mike Barnett, Angie Bumbacco — they'd all kept this from me for three months. You don't know what an achievement that is for my dad. We talked two or three times a week through that stretch. I'm surprised he didn't explode.

Now they couldn't stop telling me all the details. Apparently Pocklington had been talking about dealing me for two years. He even approached

Jerry Buss about it when Buss owned the L.A. Kings. The possible teams now had boiled down to the Kings, Detroit, the Rangers and Vancouver. Skalbania, back from the dead, was in on the Vancouver deal. He and the billionaire Jimmy Pattison would buy fifty-one percent of the Vancouver Canucks, then give me twenty-five percent. Skalbania was going to pay Pocklington $15 million for me and Peter was going to give me $2 million of it if I approved the deal. I was going to be the only person in sports history to own himself.

No wonder Skalbania had been calling me for months. And the other part of the deal was, I'd only have to play three years if I wanted and then I could become coach and general manager. One hitch: since a player can't technically be an owner, they were going to give my share to my dad until I retired. That worked out to about $10 million to my dad.

But I didn't want any part of that deal. I didn't want to leave Edmonton. I didn't want to be a coach. I knew Skalbania. He'd have me standing in Vancouver shopping malls wearing funny hats and selling tickets. Most important, I didn't want to leave the team. Put yourself in my position. Would you want to leave all of your closest friends in the world, just like that?

I knew what was behind all this. Peter's other businesses were rumored to be in serious trouble — oil, meat packing, land development, trust company, car dealership — and he needed cash. He'd sold his expensive art collection. He'd even put the Oilers up as collateral against a loan. My contract was an asset he held. In 1987, I had signed a personal services contract with him. When Peter's businesses started going south, he decided he'd take the Oilers public, the way the Boston Celtics are public. He thought it would be a great way to raise cash. After all, he'd bought the team for about $7 million and people said it was worth near $100 million now. But to go public, he needed to get me out of the personal service contract and make me the property of the team. I had him. I was on top.

I didn't nail him so much for money as for privileges. The biggest one I wrote in was that I could leave after five years and be an *unrestricted* free agent. There's supposed to be no such thing as an unrestricted free agent in the NHL — the team that gets the player is supposed to cough up big-time draft picks — but this was no-strings-attached scot-free free agency. In 1992, I'd be able to go to any team I wanted. I'd be a free man. I could sign a contract for my fair market value.

Naturally, Peter wanted me to waive the right to free agency, because that would reduce my value in a trade. Then he wanted me to sign an extension. I said I'd think about it. What I really wanted was to sign one last very big, six- or seven-year contract and end my career with Edmonton. But Peter never made us any offer. He knew what he needed and it wasn't more Stanley Cups. He didn't need to sell more tickets. His arena was already sold out. He needed cash.

While I was waiting to hear from him, I was on my honeymoon in L.A. One day the phone rang and it was Bruce McNall, the Kings owner, saying,

"Wayne, I've been given permission to talk to you."

Just like that. No call from Peter Pocklington or anyone in the organization. That was a slap in the face. I'd been loyal as hell to the Oilers, busted my butt, been part of one of the greatest dynasties in hockey history, and here I was getting thrown around from team to team like a piece of meat.

"So," said Bruce. "Do you wanna have lunch tomorrow?"

Bruce and I were acquainted. We'd had dinner a couple times in L.A. with mutual friends. I liked him. And if I was going to be traded, I liked the idea of going to L.A., where Janet could resume her career.

Bruce told me he was prepared to pay $20 million to $25 million plus three first-round draft picks and two players. In return, he'd get me and two or three other Oilers.

"Fine," I said, "As long as one of them is Marty McSorley."

I knew Slats wasn't going to give up Jari or Anderson or Mess or Kevin. And I knew the Kings needed some grit and some defense. Edmonton always had great role players for that: Pat Hughes and Kevin McClelland, Marty, Dave Hunter, Krusher, guys who would come off the bench, bust their butts, never complain and win.

Of course, I wasn't about to tell Marty or Krush. I wanted to, but if I did, the story would start leaking, the town would be all over Pocklington and he'd back out of the deal. I told my dad and my wife and that's it.

Meanwhile, I was starting to have some doubts.

This was a huge step for me and a huge risk, too. I really felt that the Oilers had at least two or three Cups left in them. That's not easy to kiss away. And what if I fell flat on my face in Los Angeles? The Kings were a team that had been running brutal for twenty years. They were eighteenth in the league that year. What if I went down there and couldn't help them a bit?

I stared at a lot of 3:00 A.M. ceilings wondering what was ahead for me. I was only twenty-seven. Janet said she was behind whatever decision I made, but she said one thing I'll never forget. "Don't underestimate your own ability."

I called Cof.

"Gretz," he said, "you'll miss the players and the friendships and the fans, but you won't even look back. It's just nice to go somewhere with a challenge."

I knew I wasn't appreciated anymore by Puck. At the awards dinner where I was to receive my eighth Hart Trophy, neither Peter nor Glen congratulated me. Nothing. Not even a handshake.

And if *that* didn't seal it for me, then what happened next did. I was in L.A., meeting with Bruce in his office, when his secretary yelled, "Mr. Pocklington for you."

Bruce always takes his calls on his speaker phone and we both knew what was going to happen next. He looked at me and I looked at him. He took the call and that's when I heard all the trash Peter was heaping on me, how I had a huge ego and how selfish I was. He even said my dad was a big pain in his side. I don't know where that came from. My dad never called Peter in all my years in Edmonton.

Now I was sure I wanted to leave. Besides, the more I got to know Bruce the more I liked him. But there was a complication. Sather was refusing to give up Marty. Pretty soon, it looked like things were falling totally apart. Peter was hedging and Glen wasn't giving up anybody. Finally I called Bruce.

"Bruce, tell Peter they gotta give up Marty or there's no deal. I'm not leaving Edmonton without Marty." I knew Slats wouldn't budge, but Peter could budge him for us.

The next morning, Bruce called Peter and said he had to have Marty and Krusher and the three draft picks had to be staggered, not consecutive. Take it or leave it.

Peter took it. Bruce gave him Carson, Martin Gelinas — the Kings' new first-round draft pick — the money and the picks. The funny thing is, all Peter got was $15 million instead of the $20 million Bruce was willing to go. And why should he have received the full price? The whole time, throughout the dealings, he kept telling Bruce what a selfish player I was.

Of course, Peter saved himself some money, too. He refused to pay me the $2 million he'd promised for okaying the deal, no matter what the deal was. "I'm not paying him, you pay him," Peter told Bruce. "I'm tired of paying him." Afterwards, everybody asked me, "How could you pass up the $2 million? You should have fought for it." But I just said, "Listen, I went home with $2 million worth of happiness."

So this was it. Bruce said to me, "Wayne, you phone Peter back now and ask to be traded and he'll do the deal tomorrow. If you don't, he might not make the trade."

So I swallowed hard and dialed up Peter that night from Bruce's office. It was about 5:00. I was sweating. I said, "Peter, I've thought a lot about it. You and I have got our differences right now. I feel that in the ten years I was there, I worked very hard. I feel that I was as loyal as any employee could be for you. But I think it's best for both of us — I'm asking you to trade me. Please trade me to L.A."

I wasn't choked up about it. I was past that. That's what Peter wanted, what he'd set as a condition of the trade — me to ask him — and I was willing to play the game. He said that the feelings were mutual and he was sorry to see me go.

Then Bruce said one more thing to me before it became a done deal.

"You know," he said, "you once told me you'd always dreamed as a kid of playing in Detroit. If you want to play in Detroit, I'll back out of the deal right now and you can go to Detroit."

Right then, I knew more than ever that I was making the right move. I told him L.A. was where I wanted to be and that was that. The next morning, Bruce faxed his signed contract to Edmonton and Peter signed it and . . . Bruce's fax broke.

The two of us almost had coronaries. What if Peter suddenly got cold feet? I was ready to get on a plane and deliver it myself.

Twenty minutes later, it was fixed and the contracts came through. I was now a King. All of a sudden, I realized I had a whole new life ahead of me.

Janet and I were shocked and excited, but we couldn't tell anybody for two weeks. The Oilers season-ticket drive didn't close until then and Peter had insisted the trade be kept secret during that time.

Bruce, his wife, Janet and I went to Chasen's that night and tried to pin the corners of our mouths down to keep from grinning. We couldn't believe it had happened. We tried to act nonchalant, but every now and then someone would walk by whom Bruce knew and he'd say, "What would you think if I got Wayne here to L.A.? Wouldn't that be something?"

"Get him out of Edmonton? Good luck."

And we'd toast our good luck.

The deal started to leak before the two weeks were up. I was staying at Alan Thicke's house while he was in Europe. Janet and I had been out to dinner. We got back about 12:30 and Bruce called at 1:00.

"We're leaving tomorrow morning at 7:00 for Edmonton," he said.

"Bruce, I don't know if I'm ready for this," I said.

And I wasn't, but we had to go. The next twelve hours looked scary.

When our private plane landed in Canada, the lady from Customs came aboard. I guess she'd heard the rumors because she looked at us and said, "Are you guys *sure* you want to do this?"

I looked Bruce right in the face and I said, "Bruce, are you sure we want to do this?"

We were sure. Mike Barnett picked us up at a private airport in Edmonton and this time the drive that I'd done hundreds of times — from the airport into the city — was one I'll never forget.

The first thing we did was go to my apartment. I wanted to tell Kevin and I wanted to tell Mess and a few other guys. Mess must have called me eight or nine times during the negotiations, but I knew I couldn't call him back. I knew if I called him, he'd go crazy and maybe talk Peter out of the deal. Mess is just that persuasive.

I made those calls while four Edmonton city policemen that Mike had arranged for stood in my apartment for my own protection. As if it wasn't wild enough, when we got to Molson House before the press conference, in walked this public relations pest hired by Peter. He said he was there to "coach me" on what to say at the press conference.

"I've written a speech for you," he said. "You might want to read it over."

Bruce and Mike were both flabbergasted, but I knew what Peter was trying to accomplish. Obviously, he was worried. In the "speech," I was supposed to tell everybody that it was all my idea, that Peter had nothing to do with it. "And then right about in here," this flack said, "would be a good time to drop in the fact that Janet's going to have your baby."

That was the last straw. I blew up. "Hey, just get out of my face!"

That's about when Peter and Glen decided they wanted to have one last private talk with me. I looked at Bruce. He looked worried. I'm sure he thought they'd try to talk me out of the whole thing.

Peter and I sat down, eye-to-eye. But it wasn't a fistfight or anything. In fact, we thanked each other for the good years. I asked him if he would take care of Joey Moss, make sure that Joey always had a job and he said he would. We shook hands and I left.

Looking back on it, the biggest mistake Peter made was not letting me just play out my four years into free agency. I refused to sign a contract that didn't have a no-trade clause in it and Peter refused to give me one that had one in it, so we were stuck. He should have let me play out the four years. As Mike Barnett put it, I would then have been a 31-year-old veteran with fourteen years on one team. I probably would have been firmly fixed in Edmonton. So Peter could've then said, "There's the door. *You* tell Edmonton you're leaving." But it never happened.

Then Glen and I sat down by ourselves. As soon as he closed the door he said, "Wayne, if you don't want to do this deal, we can call the whole thing off right now."

Despite our differences, I really don't think Glen ever wanted to trade me, but his hands were tied. He worked for Peter and Peter had to take care of the bottom line. Simple as that. Peter and I couldn't agree and he knew the deal was going through, so he fought for everything he could get. He's a hockey man, first, last and always. Although I wonder how he had the face to tell the press afterwards that he didn't know a thing about the deal.

"That trade broke my heart," he kept saying.

I did say one thing to him, though.

"I was disappointed you didn't call me through all of this. That doesn't sound very much like a coach who wants to keep a player."

"I did call," he said. "Last night."

We stood to go. "Glen," I said, "you've taught me a lot about hockey and a lot about life. I don't know if there's another man besides my father I respect as much." And I meant it. As bad as it had become between us at the end, he still had done so much for me. He believed in a small skinny center who was never where he was supposed to be, always flitting here and there, looking like he was lost. He played me a lot, even at eighteen. He understood me. If I had a big night going, he would just kind of look at me and I'd look back and he'd leave me in. He changed hockey. He was the first guy to use his four best offensive guys to kill penalties. I played a lot of minutes that way and we won a ton of hockey games that way. Is there another coach who would've gotten as much out of me? We both cried a little bit. He's a very emotional man. I am, too.

Through the glass of the office, I could see Bruce about to turn blue. So as I came out I turned my head and gave him a little wink. You could have heard him sigh in Manitoba.

The press conference was covered by everybody. Programming on the Canadian networks was interrupted to show the press conference live. My wife sat at home in L.A. and watched it by satellite. The first thing people saw was Pocklington laying it on thick. He said it was with "mixed emotions" and "a heavy heart" that he granted my request to leave the Oilers. "What do you do when an outstanding, loyal employee approaches you and asks for an opportunity to move along? You know you don't want to lose him, but at the same time, you don't want to stop him from pursuing his dreams."

Then it was my turn and I just tried to keep it simple and take the heat like I said I would. But then came the question.

"What will you remember about Edmonton?"

That question cut right to my heart. It hit me like a jolt that I was leaving my best friends and the best team in the world. Mark and Kevin and Jari and Joey and everybody. I'd joined this team, really, as a child, at seventeen — I'd literally grown up with these guys — and the roots that I was cutting off were deep. I started thinking of real basic things like scoring and congratulating each other and kidding around. Everything with us was a celebration. We were constantly celebrating something: scoring, winning, championships, records. And now, at least for me, it was about to end. I just started to cry. And every time I started to try to talk again, I couldn't. For a guy who was getting what he wanted, it sure didn't feel very good.

The date was August 9, 1988, exactly twenty-five days after my wedding.

It was also the same day workers came to my dad's house to start digging up the old backyard where I first learned to play hockey. They were putting in a present I'd given my parents. A swimming pool.

15

The Peter Principle

The day after the trade, Pocklington told an Edmonton reporter that I had "an ego the size of Manhattan" and that I was "a great actor." "I thought he pulled it off beautifully when he showed how upset he was," Peter said.

When the article appeared, Pocklington accused the writer, Jim Matheson of the *Edmonton Journal*, of misquoting him. Jim said, "Here's the tape. Listen for yourself."

Peter *had* said it, and his denial was just one more in a whole roster of lies he was handing out about me. When there had been rumors of a trade, he'd told the press, "The guys who started these rumors are full of bull."

One time, in 1987, somebody asked him if it were true that the New York Rangers were offering

$30 million for me and he said, "It's more money than you would believe."

"Why don't you do it then?" he was asked.

"There's more to life than money," said Peter.

I guess he changed his mind.

It's too bad, too. I'd liked Peter. He was a self-made millionaire with guts, an insurance salesman's son who made a ton of money in Alberta real estate, a Ford dealership, a meat-packing plant, oil and the Oilers. The problem was, I don't think he knew squat about hockey.

I remember, in about our second year in the NHL, Peter was going around shaking everybody's hand in the locker room after a big win. When he came to Marty's locker, he took a quick look at the name tag above the locker and said, "Great job, uh, uh, Marty." Then he came to Kevin's locker, shook his hand and, again, looked at the tag. Only all this tag said was "K. Lowe." So Puck says, "Great job tonight, Kenny."

To this day, when Kevin has a great game, guys will go up to him and say, "Let's see . . . two goals, two assists, another shutout. Great job there, Kenny."

He was famous for coming up with wild incentives for us to win — like the Coppertone fiasco during the WHA finals that first year — and then backing out. When I tied Marcel Dionne for the NHL scoring lead in 1980, Puck felt so guilty that my salary was dwarfed by Dionne's that he gave me a Ferrari. Or at least that's what he told everybody. The reality was that he leased me a Ferrari for three years. I had to pay the licensing and insurance on it and I had the buy out option at the end of the term. I ended up selling it and I think I lost $3,000 on the deal. Any more gifts from Peter and I was going to go broke.

When I broke Gordie Howe's all-time assist record in 1987, Peter gave me a $50,000 bond for my first-born child. I remember thinking, "This is great." Then I found out the thing *matured* at $50,000 — in twenty-five years. What that bond cost Peter was about $3,500. Two years later, Bruce gave me a savings bond too. It matured at $250,000.

When we won the Cup back in 1987, he gave us all golf clubs and a trip to Hawaii as a bonus. But, as I recall, we all got T-4s, tax bills, for the stuff. We decided the next year we wouldn't accept any gifts from Peter. Most of us already had golf clubs. What good is another set? It's just a tax bill for something you don't want.

I guess he was just trying to be generous. He could be a wonderful man, and then again sometimes he could be a complete jerk.

After we won our first Cup in 1984, Peter gave everybody diamond rings. Only the size of the diamond in your ring reflected what Peter thought you were worth to the team. That meant the trainers and the equipment guys got these tiny diamonds and the guys who sat the bench got a little bigger diamond, but not much, and so on until you-know-who got a huge one. Here we'd spent the last five years trying to bang through everybody's skull that we were a *team*, that nobody is more important than anybody else. And then Peter goes and ranks us all by carat. I didn't find out anything about it until one day Coach Muckler told me he went to get his ring appraised and the hand on the diamond meter went the wrong way. The same went for our other coach, Teddy Green. Both of them got fakes. So did all of our trainers. Is that classless or what? Sather took the coaches' rings back to Pocklington to get them genuine diamonds, and I was so embarrassed I took all the trainers' rings and had them done properly.

Sometimes you really wondered about Peter's judgment that way. When I was twenty, he was running for the leadership of Canada's Progressive Conservative Party. He wanted to win and he was not above using the team to back him. Or do you figure it was just a coincidence that his campaign colors were Oilers blue and orange? He even said in the paper, "Name me a better marketing vehicle than Gretzky and his hockey club in the Stanley Cup final." He kept after me to fly up to Ottawa with him and stand behind him as he made some speeches. How many times can you say no to your boss? I finally agreed to do it. I didn't know which shirt to wear in the morning, much less who I wanted to vote for. He lost, thank goodness.

Anyway, as I was flying back to Los Angeles with Bruce from the press conference in Edmonton, all these memories were going through my mind. I was comparing Peter to Bruce. Bruce isn't out to manipulate anybody. He is straight-up and honest. I knew that during our contract negotiations. We did it in ten minutes on that flight home.

"How much do you want to make?" Bruce asked.

First of all, you have to realize that Bruce had just made this huge deal without having signed me to a contract first. He had even said to Mike Barnett, "Geez, I'm sorry that in all the rush there was never a contract agreed upon. But I promise you I'll put Wayne in the same league with Magic, Kareem, Orel Hershiser or any of L.A.'s other top stars." Then he said something kind of interesting. He said, "You know, I've just paid $15 million for a player whose present contract gives him the right to retire in two years. You tell me, Mike, who's got the upper hand."

When Mike told me that story it blew me away. On the one hand you had Peter, pulling his hair out that I wouldn't re-sign for more than the present five years left on my contract. And on the other you had Bruce, calmly paying $15 million for what might be only two years. Who would you want to work for?

So when he said, "How much do you want to make?" I suppose I could have said, "Well, guess what? You have to pay me $20 million a year or I'm not playing." But we knew each other too well.

"I don't know," I said. "Just pay me what you think I'm worth."

"Well, help me out, I have no idea," he said. "Magic Johnson makes $3 million a year. How about that?"

"No, no," I said. "That's *way* too much."

I wasn't being humble or anything. I was trying to be smart. The Kings had lost $5 million the year before. If I was going to stick my neck and my career on the line, the last thing I wanted was for the Kings to go broke and get sold to someone I didn't know. I couldn't suck some huge amount of money out of a team that was barely staying alive.

"You want a percentage of the team?" he asked. "How about 10 percent?"

No, no. I didn't want that, either. Too much worrying.

"Look, pay me this," I said, and I wrote a number on a piece of paper.

"No, no, that's too low," he said. And he wrote a different number down.

This must have been the craziest negotiation in the history of organized sport. He was arguing my side and I was arguing his. We were sitting in the wrong chairs.

In the end, we decided on $2 million a year, base salary. Still, Bruce was a little unhappy with it. He wanted to pay me another $300,000 or so more.

"Look, take that extra that you want to pay me and spread it out over team bonuses," I said. The Kings' general manager, Rogie Vachon, ended up coming up with the plan. The team would divide up a certain amount for making the playoffs, so much for winning the Campbell Conference, so much for winning the Cup, and so on. I knew I didn't need any more money and I was a little worried about what my teammates might think about me making some gigantic salary. Maybe the team bonuses could bring us together a little. Maybe team thinking was what the Kings had been missing. Besides, I had a new goal, to bring the Stanley Cup to Los Angeles, to make hockey go in the West.

What *was* important to me in the new contract was years. I knew that I had to sign for at least six years if we were going to make people believe it would work in L.A. Plus, you know me, Mr. Hate-to-Argue, I never wanted to have to worry about a contract again. We agreed on eight years and it was done with. Bam. No apartments, no Ferraris, no personal services, nothing. I felt whole again.

Then Bruce did something I'll never forget. He called Wally and promised him that no hockey player would ever make more than me. If somebody suddenly made $4 million a year, I'd make $4,000,001. It's not in the contract, but Bruce shook my hand on it and I believe him.

I don't think I've ever met anybody like Bruce. Since that first L.A. contract, we've done a new one that rewards me even better. He insisted! Did you know his plane is Lyndon B. Johnson's old one? It's got all these fantastic security devices. If one system stops flying the plane, another one takes over. Do you realize he outbid the former president of France, Valery Giscard D'Estaing, to buy one measly little coin for $420,000, then turned around and sold it for $1 million? He's a big-time horse owner, coin collector and financial genius. And yet when you talk to him, it's like talking to your favorite uncle.

Bruce and I were going to be fine. All I had to do now was get through the next three days. The press conference in L.A. was wild. One guy who's been around said it was the biggest press turnout he'd ever seen. The gossip columnists in Canada were all blaming Janet for the trade. They were saying that she had forced me to leave Canada and move to L.A. so she could pursue her Hollywood dreams. They were calling her "Jezebel Janet" and comparing her to Yoko Ono, who, I guess, "stole" John Lennon from his adoring fans. The reporters were all over it.

I knew it was going to happen. I told Janet it was going to happen. But when you hear it, it still shocks you. And what's worse, she was pregnant and extra emotional as it was. We both knew the truth, but going through the criticism was murderous.

She cried all night that night and plenty of nights after that. She still has scars from it. We laugh about it, but I know that it hurts her to have people think that about her. What's so unfair is that she had already *made* the sacrifice to put her career on hold for me and for our baby. She'd been looking at houses for us for four months. She was making new friends. And then to have the papers rip her anyway was totally unfair and untrue.

Finally, she just blew up. She called Terry Jones of the *Edmonton Journal* and told him the truth. "Owners just don't make $15 million trades for wives," she said. "Peter Pocklington is the reason Wayne Gretzky is no longer an Edmonton Oiler. I know the real story. I know the whole story."

And when Paul Coffey broke the whole thing open in Pittsburgh the same day by saying, "No way did Wayne want to leave Edmonton," the heat started pouring in on Pocklington, regardless of what he was saying to the press.

Peter tried to tell people the trade was "a trade for the future," but nobody's that dumb. If it's a trade for the future, you go for eight first-round picks. You don't go for $15 million cash. All the cash gets you is out of hock.

This was a pretty big story in Canada. Somebody told me that the headline in the *Journal* was the biggest since the end of World War II. The *Edmonton Sun* that day had the story and then, at the bottom, a little box that said, "MORE STORIES INSIDE: PAGES 2, 3, 4, 5, 6, 10, 11, 18, 19, 23, 30, 36, 37, 38, 39, 40, 41, 42, 43, 46 AND 47."

To some Canadians, I was just one more thing the Americans had stolen. They were calling me a greedy traitor. I know it was just the flip side of their commitment as fans, but I wish they weren't so angry, and so quick to assume the worst. Some guy in the *Ottawa Citizen* predicted that I would be "buried alive" in L.A., "forgotten beneath the Magic Johnsons, the Dodgers, Hollywood and the weather itself."

Well, if there was going to be a burial, a lot of people were going to watch it. For the next five days, I did every newspaper, TV and radio station between Tijuana and Bakersfield.

Finally, Bruce called me and said, "How you doing?"

"To tell you the truth, Bruce, I'm bushed."

"Whadya say we all go spend a week lying on the beach in Hawaii?"

Did I make the right decision or what?

And as we were lying there on the beach in Hawaii with our wives and our piña coladas, I thought to myself, well, everything looks like it's going to be great. Everything is all set. Now all I have to do is keep from being the biggest flop in Hollywood since *Heaven's Gate*.

16

Hockeywood

Our house in L.A. has a long, steep, winding driveway that takes you to the front door. And it never fails that any time any of my friends from Canada visit, the first thing they say is, "Boy, you'll *never* get up that thing in the winter."

Of course, I had to make a few adjustments to life in L.A. One of them was that house. Somehow, we ended up buying a house much bigger than we wanted. I'd always been an apartment rat. All of a sudden I was living in a seven thousand-square-foot house in Encino with a swimming pool and six bedrooms, five of which I never entered. That house also came with workers. I was sitting at my kitchen table trying to eat lunch that first week when I realized there were eight people in there with me. Two maids, two gardeners, two handymen and two more guys I had no idea about.

"What do you guys do?" I asked.

"We feed the fish," they said.

I didn't even know we had fish. Turns out in the back there was some kind of fish pond with giant goldfish or something. To this day, I've only seen it once.

The maid was a piece of work, too. "How 'bout some coffee?" I asked her one day.

"Oh, no," she said. "I no know how to make the coffee. Where I come from, we no have the coffee."

"Where do you come from?"

"Colombia."

Of course. Everybody knows there's no coffee in Colombia.

Then there was the maid who was walking out into the front yard with all our sheets.

"Where are you going with the sheets?" I asked her.

"Oh," she said. "We send all the sheets to the dry cleaners."

Then there was the cook. One night before one of our first games, I asked him to make me some pasta, something to stick with me for game time.

"No, I can't do it," he says. "I have to go to the hockey game. How 'bout I make you a hot dog quick."

Where was Kevin Lowe when I needed him?

Once we got those eight people pared down to one, a man named Mario, I knew L.A. was going to be perfect for me. Actors and singers worry about "getting lost" in L.A., but that's exactly what I loved about it right off. I *could* get lost. I was a free man. I could shop, dine and drive without people stopping me, grabbing my fork or honking at me the entire way through a stoplight. The biggest difference between L.A. and Edmonton was that instead of people looking at me, I was looking at them.

There was lots to look at. A lot of Canadians, more than a million, live in L.A. — so there were more than a few fellow countrymen. Like John Candy, my favorite all-time comedian, and Michael J. Fox. Michael used to play amateur hockey himself in Vancouver, a right wing. He's like me. He wants kids and more kids.

Alan ("Growing Pains") Thicke is one of my best friends. Alan is another ex-right winger. He played at Kirkland Lake. David Foster, the Canadian musician/composer who's done tons of movie scores, is a very close friend. One night we were at a little piano bar and I said to the piano player, "Would you mind if my friend played a few of his own songs?" He said, "Why not?" And David got up and blew everybody away. He played the theme from *St. Elmo's Fire*, the theme from *The Karate Kid*, all kinds of familiar stuff. When he was done, the guy said, "You know, this guy could be good one day!"

All of a sudden hockey was getting chic in L.A. Celebrities that rivalled the famous Lakers followers started coming to our games. Overnight, season ticket sales went from four thousand to thirteen thousand. Considering that the price of the average ticket more than doubled, Bruce looked like he was going to make back his $15 million pretty quickly. He deserved it. As I said, the Kings were $5 million in the red the year before.

Now the question was, could we give the fans
something to watch?

We were bringing in a lot of new faces. There
was me, Krusher, a guy named Jim Weimer whom
Slats gave up in a different deal, our old friend
John Tonelli, whom we signed as a free agent, and
Marty, of course. Poor Marty. I never did get
around to calling him before the trade. He finally
called Mike Barnett from a golf tournament in
Maine.

"Mike, I just heard they're talking about trading
Wayne. You've got to give me Puck's number. I've
got to stop the deal!"

"Marty," said Mike. "Are you sitting down? The
deal is done...."

"Oh, no! I can't believe it! This is the stupi-
dest...."

"And you're going with him!"

To this day, Marty insists that Krusher and I got
traded for Jimmy Carson and Martin Gelinas and
he got traded for the $15 million.

I could tell right away that our problem was
going to be at right wing. We didn't have anybody
who was going to make people forget Jari. I played
with Sylvain Couturier and Bob Kudelski and Jay
Miller and Paul Fenton, too, a guy they called up
from our farm team in New Haven.

You'd have been amazed at how many guys we
called up from New Haven that year. Our head
coach, Robbie Ftorek, loved New Haven. He kept
bringing up these guys from New Haven to play my
right wing. Bernie would always go around saying,
"OK, guys, did you hear about the Player of the
Week contest they're running in New Haven? First

prize is a trip to Disneyland and a week on Wayne's line."

The first loss, I'm looking around thinking, "These guys don't look too upset." In Edmonton, it would have been chaos. Glen Sather would have been measuring everybody for nooses. I knew then that the first thing we had to do was turn that attitude around.

There were other things I noticed. It was hard to be close to your teammates in L.A. Edmonton isn't big so nobody lived more than twenty minutes from anybody else. While I was an Oiler, we made it a team rule that you had to meet at a local restaurant at least once or twice a week for lunch after practice. But in L.A., some guys live in Van Nuys and other in Hermosa Beach. That's an hour-and-a-half drive from each other. And with L.A. traffic, nobody's going to be sitting around in the afternoon shooting the breeze. They were gone.

Our practice facility in Culver City was one of the coldest I'd been in. That might be OK in Winnipeg or Boston but when you come out of that into a ninety-degree Los Angeles day, it's a great way to get sick. No wonder we led the leagues in colds. That will lose you a few more games.

I got along fine with Ftorek, but he wore the wildest sweaters in the history of Dacron. Crazy orange and purple jobs. One time he had on a wool one that was so ugly somebody said there were sheep protesting outside the Forum. Among the other changes, it seems like we had a new assistant captain every week, which let Bernie Nicholls remark that the Kings were the only team with a

Velcro "A" so Robbie could move it from one guy to another without having to take out all the thread.

When our first game arrived, I was nervous. I hadn't been that nervous since my first All-Star game. The Forum was buzzing. This was Big Time. They had Roy Orbison singing the national anthem, if you can believe that. We were playing Detroit and the stands were loaded with stars. It was a sellout. Mike Downey, the columnist for the *Los Angeles Times*, called it "Hockeywood." Magic Johnson sent balloons. It felt like the start of something.

Things always happen to me when the lights are the brightest and everybody's holding their breath. On my first shot in my first game in a new uniform in this new arena in this new town with all these new people watching, I scored a goal. What is it they say in Hollywood? Cut. That's a wrap.

It was a five-on-three, Dave Taylor gave me a perfect pass just to the right of the goalmouth and all I had to do was shoot it in. Guess who I beat? My old friend Greg Stefan. Small world. We beat them, 8–2, and I got three more assists besides. Lucky Luc had a hat trick and we were off. We got the Kings off to their best start ever, winning our first four games.

I knew hockey had pretty much captured L.A. the night we were playing the Flyers and the Dodgers were playing the Oakland Athletics in their first home game of the World Series. We sold out.

We didn't play much defense, but we were far and away the highest scoring team in the league. It

was so much fun for me and I think the other players were having fun, too. The year before these
guys had played to zero sellouts on the road. That
year, they played to thirty. Hockey's more enjoy-
able when fans are watching.

Sooner or later I had to go to the one place I
really wanted to avoid. On October 19, 1988, we
were playing in Edmonton. It was a game I dreaded. We were either going to beat some of my best
friends in the world or they were going to blow us
out and make Bruce and me look stupid. Either
way, I knew there was no way it was going to be a
good feeling when I left.

I saw Sather before the game and he didn't say a
word to me. He's pretty honest that way. I didn't
exist because I was on the other team now. He's
not phony about it. He didn't come around and
want friendly pictures taken with me or act like we
were best buddies the way Pocklington did that
day.

I remember walking on the ice, watching the
Oilers warm up and getting this weird feeling that I
was standing in the wrong end of the rink.

I got two assists that night, but we lost 8–6. I
also got a pretty good bruise from Mess. I told
reporters before the game I thought Mess would
check me, but I was wrong. He steamrolled me,
backed up and steamrolled me again. The guy is a
competitor and this was a game he wanted to win.
I didn't hold it against him. Now I know why people cringe at the sight of him.

My next trip to Edmonton was happier. It was
for the All-Star game, my tenth in a row. Jari and I

picked up right where we left off, as if I'd only been on a long vacation. It was the same old thing: the less we handled the puck, the better we were. I got a goal, two assists (one to Jari) and the MVP car, which was the one I gave to Semenko. I wonder what he thought when they delivered the car and it was Kings' silver and black? *Gretz, you and I are going on a canoe ride.*

That night was full of emotion for me. I was sitting there in the first period with Mess and Kevin and Jari, just like the old days. But at the same time, I knew it would never be the same again. That felt a little sad.

The Kings, however, were playing great. By the time we got to the All-Star break, we were 24–15–1, by far the best first half of a Kings' season in years. Bernie was playing like a madman and I wasn't too bad, either.

We were playing one night in Detroit. By the end of the second period, I had five points — a goal (the 600th of my career) and four assists. My best ever was eight points in a game so I felt hot. But at the end of the second period, Detroit's Yzerman stripped the puck from me and scored easily. I was so mad I broke my stick over the back of the goal post. We were leading 5–0 when it happened, so it wasn't a felony or anything, but Robbie got in my face. "Wayne, I'm benching you. I can't stand for that."

I sat out for two shifts in the third period, came back in and got another assist. But the rumors that started were unbelievable. The story was that Robbie had said, "Wayne, I've got to teach you a lesson." And I supposedly said, "Robbie, we're trying to win a Stanley Cup here. If you want to teach, go back to New Haven."

I never said it.

Robbie did some other odd things. He had some talented guys in that camp whom I knew could play, guys like Doug Crossman, who made the 1987 Canada Cup team. But as the season unfolded, Crossman didn't play. Robbie had decided to let Brian Maxwell, his assistant coach, handle the defense lock, stock and barrel. Whatever Brian said, went. Brian didn't play Crossman. Nobody could figure it out.

On the other hand, Robbie was a great teacher of the game and he was great with young players. He loves the underdog. Robbie wasn't afraid to give kids from our minor league franchise in New Haven a chance. The problem was he'd do it to a fault.

I admire Robbie's compassion for young guys, but I'm not sure loving the underdog is a trait that gets you points in the NHL. Clearly, we needed a coach who could handle veterans, a coach's coach. Robbie wasn't that guy. And since he hated dealing with the press, the press hated him back. Pretty soon, their game was, "Let's get Robbie fired." And they succeeded. But we had a damn good year, even though I couldn't help feeling that with a veteran coach we could have gone further. People want to make Robbie and me out to be blood enemies. We weren't. We were friends. When I broke Gordie's record the first call I got was from Robbie.

We ended up 42–31–7 and took second place in

our division. We were twelve victories and twenty-three points better than the year before. We went from eighteenth place in the league to fourth. It was one of the biggest turnarounds in hockey history and one of the most satisfying seasons in my life. And the best was yet to come.

We opened the playoffs against, you guessed it, Edmonton. This was tricky. I wanted like crazy to win that series, but at the same time, I didn't want my buddies, the Stanley Cup defending champions, to lose. I never enjoyed a minute of it. I spent nine years with these guys and yet, during the whole series, fifteen days, we never spoke once. It was awful.

The series opened in L.A. and everything I'd ever said about Grant Fuhr was true. Twice he stopped me cold from point blank. We lost it 4–3. But our guy, Kelly Hrudey, wasn't so bad, either. He stood on his head to help us win Game Two, 5–2. On to Edmonton and a shutout loss in Game Three. Mess killed us. He laid out a perfect cross-ice pass to Jimmy Carson to set up the game-winning goal. Now we were down two games to one and Pocklington was big-timing all the writers. "The people of Edmonton told me from the beginning it was a good trade," he said.

Mess beat us again in Game Four. With the game tied at 3–3 and only a minute left, he bore down on Hrudey, even though he was wearing Taylor on his back, and jammed a shot off Kelly that was rebounded in by Steve Smith.

As we were riding back on the plane that night, down three games to one, I got up and told everybody, "We've got 'em right where we want 'em!" I think the only one who believed me was me.

We won Game Five, 4–2, and somehow won Game Six back in Edmonton 4–1. We were down 1–0 when Allison tied it with a fantastic play from behind the net. Then Weimer scored what would be the winning goal to make it 2–1.

Which brought us to the big game, Game Seven, a chance to knock off the two-time defending Stanley Cup champions. The town was going bonkers. People who used to think ice was only good for making daiquiris were driving around with Kings pennants on their Jaguar antennas. Everybody was freaked out about it. Everybody, that is, except my houseman, Mario. All Mario cares about is getting his work done and listening to his Spanish Bible verses on his Walkman. I've never been quite sure he understands what I do. As I was heading for the Forum that night, he stopped me and said, "Where are you going, Wayne?"

"Uh, I'm going to the rink now, Mario. It's Game Seven tonight."

"That's nice."

At least he didn't want a ticket. I'd already spent $7,000 on playoff tickets that year, in case you think we get them for free.

I got the first goal fifty-two seconds into the first period, a squibber that got past Grant. From then on it was manic hockey. Jari scored for them. Chris Kontos scored for us. Simpson scored for them. Bernie for us. Kevin for them. It was 3–3 with four minutes left in the second period when Edmonton got into a two-man disadvantage with penalties and I hit Bernie who jammed it in for a 4–3 lead.

We should have made it 5–3 to start the third period but John Tonelli hit the center pipe down the back of the goal and the puck bounced twenty feet out. All the TV replays showed it was a goal, but it happened so fast the goal judge didn't see it. Andy Van Hellemond, the referee, sure saw it. He gave them a cheapo holding penalty right away (on the bench, we call it a "Revlon," a makeup call). On the power play, Dale DeGray, our defenseman, got a goal right away. They should've given the assist to Tonelli.

When I got the last goal of the night, an empty-netter with a minute and a half left, it was 6–3 and it was over. It was also Bruce's thirty-ninth birthday and he looked like he was ready to cry. People have called that series win a fluke, but they've forgotten that we beat Edmonton the last three times we met in the regular season.

After the game, I finally talked to Mess and Kev, but I could hardly say anything. I knew just how they felt. Here they'd had us down 3–1 and they'd lost. People don't know what they went through. There was more going on that week than hockey. They played that series under some big pressure from the media, what with the trade and all.

We got swept by Calgary in the next series, but I think it was sort of the way our second Edmonton team upset Montreal and then got beat by the Islanders. There are only so many miracles in a new hat.

And even though I ended up with 168 points compared to Mario Lemieux's 199, I was voted my ninth Hart Trophy as the MVP. Mario wasn't happy. "Nothing in this league makes sense," he told the papers. "In the past, they gave it to the best player or top scorer. I don't know why it should change." I think maybe Mario was misquoted a little. His English occasionally goes awry. But I didn't care. That Hart Trophy was the sweetest because of what I'd put on the line: my reputation. And it felt sweet because of what I'd contributed to my new team. I think that's what athletes need more than anything: a cause, a *need* to keep proving themselves, over and over again.

The sweetest part might have been proving it to Peter. He never figured I'd make an impact in L.A. That's the reason he was willing to let me go there in the first place. He'd have *never* allowed a trade to a contender. He sent me to the worst team in the division because he figured that at best I'd help them from awful to sort-of-awful. I guess he underestimated us all.

17

A Bloody Shame

Hockey is the only team sport in the world that actually *encourages* fighting. I have no idea why we let it go on. The game itself is so fast, so exciting, so much fun to watch, why do we have to turn the ice red so often? Why do the best shots in a game have to be on somebody's nose instead of somebody's net?

Figure this one out: You can accidentally high-stick a guy and get thrown out of a game, but two guys can stand there and beat each other dizzy and not be thrown out of the game. What sense does that make? In fact, they can stand there and beat each other to a pulp *twice* in a game and not be thrown out.

In Edmonton, the Oilers actually had some guys

take boxing lessons. Marty McSorley did and so did Semenko and Kevin McClelland. I can't blame them. If the league is going to allow mayhem to go on, you might as well be able to defend yourself.

All right, I know what you're thinking. *We know why Gretzky wants to get rid of fighting. There's nobody in the league he can beat.* And, of course, you'd be right. I think I've been involved in three fights in my life and have gone 0–0–3.

When a fight breaks out, the first thing I do is look for a little guy I can grab. They're easy to find because they're looking for me. Neither one of us particularly likes the thought of having any more new teeth. Before the game, I tell my teammates exactly who I want on the other side when the fight breaks out. I always used to look for Pierre Larouche, or Winnipeg's Thomas Gradin. Now it's Jari. Then we just sort of hold onto each other by the shoulders and ask if we're going to each other's charity golf tournament, how's the family, very nice, how's business, great. Oops, watch it. They're coming this way. And then when it's done, "OK, nice to see you again."

The worst it ever got was the night with Doug Lecuyer of Chicago. He was playing me really tight and hitting me a lot, so I dropped my gloves and hit him. I don't think I hit him very hard. In fact, I think it was the surprise of the thing that shook him. Finally, he just sort of grabbed me and threw me down and said, "OK, just hold on. I won't hit you." And I said, "Sounds good to me." And that was it. We each got a five-minute penalty for waltzing.

People always ask me, "Are hockey fights for real?" Yes, they're real. If they weren't, I'd get in more of them.

I know fights bring some people into the building. Fights probably bring a lot of people into the building. But how many people do they keep *out* of the building? I've met people in L.A. who say, "Well, we don't go to the games because it's too violent." To me, that's just sad. If hockey is ever going to become accepted all over the continent, we have to start convincing the American public that it's a great sport. And it's not convincing anybody as long as the guy on the eleven-o'clock news can show highlights of a hockey fight instead of a hockey goal.

Have you ever noticed that during the playoffs the number of fights goes down to about zero? And that's when our best hockey is played. If that isn't proof that we don't need fighting, I don't know what is. In the proposed Global Hockey League, fighting will be totally illegal and players can once again decide whether they want to wear helmets or not. If a guy isn't wearing a helmet, the fans can identify with him a little better and I think it helps build fan loyalty.

But in the archaic world of the NHL, the fighting rolls on. The depressing thing is, as much as I've talked about this, I've made absolutely zero progress on it. Every time I bring it up to the league, they point to these studies about how many people want fighting.

I realize there are a lot of people's jobs at stake here, guys who are in the league only because they can fight, but there are fewer than people think. Marty, for instance, could be in this league if fighting were illegal. The same was true for Semenko. And when it gets right down to it, I don't think even *those* guys want to fight. They didn't go through all those years of Pee Wee and Bantam and Junior just to come to the big-time and play Mike Tyson on skates. No kid I've ever heard of skates around on the pond dreaming, "Here's Billy in the Stanley Cup final! He's knocking the brains out of that guy!"

The way to do it is by cleaning up junior hockey first. Make it an immediate ejection for anybody fighting and a two-game suspension. It's got to start there. We've got to stop breeding animals. I don't want to see any more fourteen-year-olds drop their sticks and gloves and start fighting. That's not hockey.

There are times when I wonder if the people who can do something about fighting — and the rest of the league's problems — have any idea what they're doing. Mostly what I think they're obsessed with is the bottom line. I remember when I had the great year in 1982, I got an invitation to do the "Tonight Show" with Johnny Carson. We were in Toronto and we had a day off, so I figured I could fly to L.A., do the show and be back in time for the game. The problem was, I had to go through Chicago to get to L.A., and Chicago was snowed in. There was no way in or out. So I thought, well, this is a pretty big deal, why not rent a plane and fly directly to California? The NHL would arrange it, I thought. I mean, how many NHL players had ever appeared on Carson? I thought it was a chance to talk about hockey and do the league some real good. You can't *buy* that kind of exposure.

So I phoned the league office and told them what we needed. They wouldn't lift a finger. When I offered to pay half the expense of the jet myself they still wouldn't lift a finger.

Sometimes, the fans get hurt because the league drops the ball. As part of the 89–90 All-Star game, the league sold tickets to the practice that was held the day before the game. They filled the arena. Sounds good, doesn't it? Except they forgot to tell all the players, and since that practice is usually optional, seven of us missed it. I felt awful, because I take great pride in not missing engagements.

The P.A. announcer at the arena said, "Ladies and gentlemen, Wayne Gretzky is not in the building. We don't know where he is. Only *he* knows why he isn't here." I'd like to thank him for that. He must be a classy guy. The fans were so upset by game time that they booed every time I touched the puck. I guess it doesn't count that I took two hours to do an interview with NBC that afternoon to plug the game, the city and the league.

It's like the deal on Soviet players. I still don't understand why the NHL clubs pay the Soviet Sports Federation hundreds of thousands to get player releases. If they want to play here, fine, they're more than welcome, but nobody paid my parents $500,000 to release *me*. I mean, why does a New Jersey or a Calgary pay $300,000–$400,000 to the Soviets for thirty-year-old Russians, yet all a junior team gets for a budding NHL star is $40,000?

The junior franchises are having a tough time

staying afloat and I should know. I've owned two of them, Belleville and now Hull in Quebec. I have the best franchise in Canada in junior hockey and I'm losing money. I've owned Hull for three years, won three championships and I'm $337,000 in the hole. I get letters from the president of the league saying, "You can't say that stuff," but it's true. The U.S. colleges are taking many of the best players because kids get the chance to go to school in case their hockey career doesn't work out. That makes sense, but if the junior franchises start folding, hockey is in serious trouble. Junior hockey is the backbone of the Canadian game.

Not that the NHL itself is in any great shape. The old teams — Montreal, Chicago, Toronto — have a lot of power. In almost any fight, those teams will win and the "newer" teams, like L.A., will draw the short end of the stick, especially in scheduling.

That's why I'm hereby volunteering my ten-point plan to revamp the NHL. There's no charge.

1. *End the fighting.* Make it illegal. Period. If you fight, you're out of the game.

2. *Expand.* The NHL is going into the San Francisco area next year. Great. Now expand to Seattle, Houston and maybe Milwaukee.

3. *Rename the conferences.* It's parochial to call them the Wales Conference and the Campbell Conference. And it doesn't much help to have the Adams, Norris, Smythe and Patrick Divisions. We

have enough trouble trying to explain the blue line to people. Just call them East and West.

4. *Realign the conferences.* Everybody wants to blame the president, John Ziegler, for the NHL's problems, but he's pretty good. The trouble is that some of the owners always do only what's best for their own team, not for the game. For instance, the lineup of the conferences is ridiculous, but it's set up so that Toronto and Chicago are almost guaranteed to make the playoffs. What should be done is put ten teams in one conference and eleven in the other. As it is now, we play teams in our own conference eight times — which is way too many — and the other teams three times. The new way, we'd play them six and three, respectively. More people would see more players and therefore build interest. Forget the divisions. Keep the playoffs the same and eventually have the two conference winners play the Stanley Cup.

5. *Bring on free agency.* Why shouldn't we fight for it? Free agency hasn't hurt any other professional sport. It's only helped baseball. Now football is getting it. Look at the Green Bay Packers. They rebuilt their team mostly from Plan B free agents. If the players wanted to strike for it, I'd strike. The fans don't know it, but it'd be the best thing for the game.

6. *Institute a week-off plan.* By the end of February, the players are so spent that the fans and the owners don't get out of us all that they could. The

owners have us running all over the country doing exhibition games before the season, then the All-Star game (which now includes an extra day of "skills" competition and if you don't participate in the skills, you can't play in the game) halfway through the season, then the playoffs at the end of the season. That's over one hundred days of hockey sometimes. How many years does it take off your career? Give the players a break. Give each team five consecutive days off (not counting travel days) in January or February. You never have more than two teams taking the time off at once, so you don't have to shut down anything. The league just keeps right on going. When the players come back, they're playing better and everybody is getting their money's worth.

7. *Let the players help make the rules.* In the NHL, the people making the rules usually never played the game. For instance, the league sneaked through a rule last year that let only "official suppliers' " logos appear on the skates, sticks, and gloves we use. The players have to use the "official" stuff because the league wanted the new revenue. If we want to use another stick or a different glove that isn't "official," we have to obliterate the name with Magic Marker. Guess how long the players will keep getting their tailored sticks from the suppliers if the logos are removed before we can go on the ice? Of course, we can always use the "official" stuff. . . .

The league does some surprising things when money is involved. In 1988, there was a company in Japan that was going to pay Bruce $1 million to bring us there to train for ten days and play two exhibition games, all expenses paid. Apparently the International Committee of the NHL killed the deal. The NHL was angry that it wasn't getting a cut. Never mind that Bruce had lost millions and risked millions more to build an NHL franchise in a tough market with lots of other championship teams, and had even, in the end, offered them a cut.

8. *Pay the refs more.* The top referee in the entire league makes something like $85,000. An everyday linesman makes $30,000. If you want the best ref-ereeing, you've got to pay the price. I mean, would you want to break up those fights?

9. *Bring back ESPN.* When the NHL chose Sports Channel America over ESPN, it was another decision by the league to choose the quick buck over long-term effects. Sure, we got more money from Sports Channel, but how much did we lose in exposure? Who sees Sports Channel, anyway? I'll tell you who, only one in ten U.S. homes, that's who. ESPN, who had bought the NHL rights before Sports Channel outbid them, goes into fifty-one million homes. Obviously, the NHL's decision was based upon what was better for the owners' pocket-books, not what was better for the game. What a shocker.

10. *Let us play in the Olympics.* Every three or four years the NHL's best players give up seven

weeks of their summer to play in an international tournament — the Canada Cup. Granted it makes the Players Association a lot of money — mainly because the players ask for only nominal compensation. But the Canada Cup was created also as an alternative to the Olympics since the NHL pros weren't allowed in the Olympic Games. Now the Olympic rules allow us to play. The NHL doesn't. If our stars played in the Olympics they would be seen in new markets that might stimulate interest and new followers of hockey. Eventually the sport could truly be national in the United States and network television might come calling.

Any questions?

18

It's Howe, Not How Many

It was eerie how all the roads in my life kept leading back to Edmonton: the All-Star game there in 1988, then the playoff, then, in August of 1988, the unveiling of a statue of me in front of the Northlands Coliseum. But in October of 1989 came the most incredible coincidence of all.

Start with the statue. The city wanted to put something up for me in the wake of the trade. I didn't want it. I fought not to have it, but they wouldn't take no for an answer. I appreciated the honor, but I wanted them to wait until I was retired. I have enough trouble trying to get people to treat me like a normal person without having some statue staring at them on the way into the arena. First, they wanted to name some artificial waterfall after me. I said no. Then they wanted to name the street after me. I wasn't comfortable with that, either. I said I was a hockey player, not a politician. That's when they came up with the idea of a statue. They asked me how I wanted it to look. All I said was if there was going to be a statue, I wanted it to stand for what meant most to me, that we were champions. They said they'd work on it.

But when the city was ready to unveil it, the Oilers' management refused to participate. Sather said it was "against club policy" to honor a former player before he retires. The club is only twelve years old. How many statues are we talking about here?

By that time I had promised the city I'd come and I wasn't going to back out. But I made up my mind that I wasn't going up there again for any more events. Nothing. If the Oilers' management want to retire my jersey or have some kind of reunion, they'll have to do it without me. If they didn't want to be there for my official "day" in Edmonton, that was their choice. But I wasn't coming back.

The day before the unveiling was the funeral of one of our best friends, Susan Mah, the daughter of the owner of my favorite restaurant in Edmonton. Susan Mah was one of the kindest, hardest-working people I knew and then she was struck down by cancer right in the best years of her life. Susan's tragedy made me feel even more uncomfortable about having this huge statue put up. Where was her statue?

Not only that, but I was worried about death threats. Some nut wanted to kill me on my wedding day in Edmonton and I was still an Oiler then.

Now I was wearing a different uniform, had been called disloyal and had helped kick the Oilers out of the playoffs. A big parade was planned and I was supposed to ride with Janet in a convertible. I was scared for me and for my family.

On the big day my friends showed up, policy or no policy: Mess, Kevin, Semenko, Dave Hunter, Charlie Huddy, Steve Smith, a lot of guys. Guys who don't let team politics come between friendships. The parade came off without a hitch and when we got to the Coliseum, I was shocked. They'd sold it out. They even had seats on the floor and they'd sold those out. I was starting to get a little shaky.

It meant a lot to hear from the people directly. Some of the press and Pocklington had made people think I'd abandoned the Oilers, but, in the end, the fans came around to the truth. They weren't talking about my wife dragging me out of town anymore. Now they were talking about dragging Pocklington out of town and lynching him. For some reason, hearing those cheers that day made up for all the time when I was wondering if all the good will I'd built up with the fans had disappeared just because Pocklington got a few lies printed in the paper.

Even people who had been caught up in all the accusations came to me that day and said they were sorry. Hey, I understood. You see something in the paper and you automatically believe it's true. And when a reporter gets an outrageous quote from Pocklington, it's hard to decide not to run it.

I knew the trade had been an emotional time for me, but I guess I didn't realize it was emotional for the fans, too. Janet told me, in the middle of it all, that I should be happy the fans were feeling something, even if it was anger, because it meant they cared for me, that they didn't want to lose me. She said the fans would come around. At the time, I couldn't see it. But on that day in Edmonton, surrounded by all of them, it became crystal clear.

I was holding up fine until they gave me a picture of three little kids playing ice hockey on a pond, with the skyline of the city in the background. One kid in the picture is going home and the other two kids are waving goodbye. Then I realized it was me leaving and Kev and Mess waving goodbye.

Then they unveiled it: a six-foot-high bronze statue of me holding the Stanley Cup above my head. It was one of the most chilling moments of my life. When I looked at it, I wasn't embarrassed like I thought I would be. I was elated. It represented what the *team* had done. I was proud of it. And they announced they were going to put it by an entrance that I knew Slats and Peter Puck use every day. Maybe they'll look up at it sometimes and wonder what might have been if they hadn't broken that team up.

All I had to do was make one speech — and I got Joey to come up and do that for me — and it was over. I was relieved and I felt sort of whole again. Edmonton is in my blood. That's where I played my greatest years, made my greatest friends, found the greatest memories. I still want it to be a home.

When I was a kid, I wanted to play, talk, shoot,

walk, eat, laugh, look and be like Gordie Howe. He was far and away my favorite player. I had his autographed picture on my wall. One time I went to the barber shop and asked for a haircut *exactly* like Gordie's, even down to the little bald spot on his head. I had the barber cut all the hair off at the same place Gordie was losing his, then I had him pile the rest of my hair up on the side Gordie piled his up on. If they could've given me some crow's feet and smashed out a couple of teeth, I'd have been the happiest kid alive.

Every day my mom didn't steal it and throw it in the wash, I wore my authentic Detroit Red Wings number 9 sweater, the one that made me sweat and itch all the time. To this day, if I see a kid wearing a number 99 sweater, I'll try to give him a puck or something, because I know what it meant to me to meet Gordie when I was a kid.

When I met him the first time I was eleven years old. Gordie was giving me an award at a Kiwanis banquet. Beforehand, he told me something I never forgot: "Kid, keep practicing that backhand. Someday, it's going to be an important shot."

Gordie bailed me out of a serious jam that day. I told everybody beforehand that I couldn't get up there to speak, no way. Naturally, the M.C. introduced me like I was going to speak. I was starting to cry when Gordie whispered in my ear, "Go up there and say, 'I'm sorry, but I'm lost without a pair of skates,' and walk off." So I went up there and . . . totally forgot what I was supposed to say. So Gordie came up to the microphone and said, "When someone has done what this kid has done, he doesn't have to say anything."

Gordie Howe was cool. Not only was he this great player who scored more than anybody else, he *looked* cool, with his hair always perfectly slicked back and those eagle eyes staring holes in people. I used to love to watch when somebody hit Gordie with a cheap shot. He wouldn't get them back right away — very uncool — but later, when the guy wasn't paying attention, *wham*, Gordie would wipe him out with a massive check.

Gordie was great at clinics. One time, he put on the most incredible display of stick-handling anyone had ever seen. He came on the ice, and using the butt end of the stick, he went all over the rink, moving the puck in and out of the reach of all the kids trying to get him. Finally, he stopped against the boards and turned the stick right side up, puck and all. He'd nailed the puck to the end of the stick.

My dream was to someday play a game with Gordie and it came true in 1979 at the WHA All-Star game. I really didn't expect to play much, and I felt kind of dumb because the jersey they gave me was about two miles too big. It might have fit Semenko, but not me. Gordie saw it and said, "Come with me." We went back into the trainer's room and he took a needle and thread and actually sewed it to make it smaller and tighter for me. I still have that sweater at home, with Gordie's stitchwork in it.

Then the coach for that game, Jacques Lemaire, came up and told me, "You're gonna center Gordie and Mark (Gordie's son)." As we sat there on the bench, I said to Gordie, "Boy, I'm really nervous about this game." He kind of yawned, stretched and said, "Yeah, so am I." That cracked me up and calmed me down. Then he said, "Look, when they drop the puck (at the opening faceoff), get it back to the defenseman. He'll give it back to you, then you dump it into my corner and get it in front of the net." So that's exactly what I did and we scored in about ten seconds. If I had played with Gordie Howe my whole life I'd have 3000 points by now.

That same year, after the regular season, we played together in the WHA All-Star game series against the Moscow Dynamo. There was this one Soviet who wouldn't stop hooking and chopping at me. I didn't know what to do about it, so Gordie said, "The next time down the ice, when you see him coming, flush him off to the right and get the hell out the way." So that's what I did and when I looked back, the Soviet was laying flat on his butt, half out of it. Whatever Gordie did, I'm glad I didn't have to watch it.

I've always felt Gordie and I have been linked in some way by fate. The day I won my first Hart Trophy is the exact same day Gordie retired. By the end of that first season with the Kings, I was thirteen points behind Gordie's all-time points record of 1,850. But, to be honest, I had mixed feelings about that record. It was the one record I wasn't sure I wanted to break. He's the best player ever and a part of me felt he should be remembered as having the most points ever.

Besides, Gordie wasn't just about points. He won the Hart Trophy six times. He played in five decades. He was one of the top five scorers in the

NHL twenty straight years. When he was forty-eight years old he was MVP of the WHA. Jack Nick-laus won the Masters at forty-six, but was he Player of the Year at forty-eight? Gordie played in an All-Star game when he was fifty-one. I know I won't be playing in an All-Star game when I'm fifty-one. I'll be laying on a beach in Tahiti watching Gordie play in it.

Anyway, it was either break the record or quit. Before the schedule for the 1989–90 season came out, I figured I would probably get that fourteenth point in the sixth game of the season. When they showed me the schedule, a chill went up my spine. Game Six: at Edmonton.

But my premonition was looking false. By the time we got to Vancouver for the fifth game, I still needed four points just to tie. It was pretty clear that nobody thought I was going to get four against Vancouver. Gordie was there and he didn't even wear his suit. My parents didn't even show up. They were right, but I got three, including the game-winner with one second left.

Now it looked like I *was* going to break it in Edmonton instead of L.A., much to the displeasure of my wife and Bruce. I told them to blame our general manager, Rogie Vachon. Why Rogie? Because it was Rogie who was playing goalie against Gordie his last night, April 6, 1980. If Rogie had let in two more goals, we could've broken the thing in L.A.

When I got to Edmonton, I locked myself in my room and took the phone off the hook. Everybody wanted to talk about the irony of the whole thing.

I'll admit, it was rich. Me, back in Edmonton to break the biggest record in hockey in somebody else's uniform while Peter Pocklington tried to smile about it all. Plus, the day before, Jimmy Carson, the key guy in the trade, had quit the Oilers. I guess there are shadows everywhere you go.

The game began and I got an early assist to tie the record. All I needed was one more to set a new one. Naturally, the whole time I was on the ice, Tik was in my ear with his same old stupid rap: "Come on Gretz, you can do it tonight! Got to get the record tonight, Gretz! Can you do it?"

In the second period, the Oilers' Jeff Beukeboom laid a massive hit on me, massive but clean. Jeff carried no grudge. In fact, he was one of the Oilers who defied Sather and came to the statue unveiling. But I was real woozy for a while, just the same. Our new coach, Tom Webster, came real close to sending me back to the locker room. He gave me some rest in the third period and that helped, although I think I was still a little dizzy.

We were down 4–3 when Webby called a timeout with three minutes left in the game. The Edmonton fans started chanting *Gretz-ky! Gretz-ky!* Webby let me stay on the ice the rest of the time, partly for the record, partly because we needed the win.

Then, with about one minute left, our defenseman, Steve Duchesne, stole Kevin's clearing attempt at the blue line and drove it back into our own zone. Usually in that case, I'd go behind the net, but for whatever reason, maybe I was still dizzy, I came out and stood in front of it. Or maybe, like my dad says, these things are pre-planned by a higher authority. On nights this big, even my mistakes seem to be the right move. The puck hip-hopped over the top of Kevin's stick, bounced off Dave Taylor's knee and squirted right in front of me. There it was, History Puck, just staring at me. All I did was backhand it over Edmonton's sprawled-out goalie, Bill Ranford, high into the top half of the net.

The first thing I remember thinking is, "We tied 'em!" But a fraction of a second after that, it hit me. "The record!" I started skating around wildly, looking for somebody's arms to jump into. Luckily, Larry Robinson, 6'4", was available.

They stopped the game and everybody came down, my wife, Bruce, my dad, Gordie, his wife. Gordie whispered in my ear, "Congratulations." Mess gave me a solid-gold bracelet, with diamonds, on behalf of the Oilers. Then Larry and Dave Taylor gave me a crystal hologram from the Kings. Then the NHL commissioner, John Ziegler, gave me a silver tea tray with the logos of all twenty-one teams engraved on it. Even the New Jersey Devils. I got up and could hardly remember anything I said. I think I said, "This is the greatest feeling in the world."

But it wasn't the gifts, it was the moment. What were the odds of me breaking the biggest record in my life with everybody who was close to me, everybody who meant anything to me, good or bad, right on the ice with me? All my friends were there, even Sather, who had believed in me enough to play me at such a young age.

There was one more guy in the stands that night,

Krusher. He wasn't scheduled to be on the road trip because he had a cast on his hand. He bought his own ticket and flew up just to see it happen. That meant a lot to me. Krusher stands 6'2" and weighs about 210, but when I got the goal, he looked like a little kid with those tears in his eyes. He almost got me crying.

They wanted me to do one of those instant, "After this, I'm going to Disneyland" ads, but I refused. I didn't want to be doing a commercial in the middle of a hockey game. I don't think that at the moment of your greatest achievements, your happiest times, you should be worrying about endorsement contracts.

As for the game, Webby left me in for the overtime. I felt bad for Kevin and Mess because I *knew* we were going to win and we did. And guess who got the game winner? Robinson fed Tonelli along the end board, slipped it to me and I backhanded it past Ranford's glove into the corner of the net and we won. This was almost too perfect.

Two goals, two backhands. In fact, when you think about it, almost every important goal I've ever scored has been a backhand — my first WHA goal, my first NHL goal and now these two. You were right, Mr. Howe.

After the game, my dad looked like he'd been on a fifty-mile hike. I don't know how much more of this stuff he can take.

"Wayne," he said, lighting up a cigarette. "How *do* you do things like that?"

"It's simple, Dad," I said. "We had to win the game."

Bruce had a few more gifts up his sleeve that

next game at home two nights later. First, he gave me a LeRoy Neiman painting of me in a Kings uniform. Then he gave Gordie 1,850 silver coins and me 1,851 gold ones — worth about $300,000. And guess what? No tax bill ever came, either. Bruce paid 'em.

Something else eerie happened. It turns out that if I hadn't broken the record in Edmonton, I'd have broken it two nights later in L.A. — the day of the tragic San Francisco earthquake, and who could have celebrated that night?

Back in the locker room that night in L.A., there was a telegram waiting:

> CONGRATULATIONS ON THIS TREMENDOUS MILESTONE IN YOUR CAREER. BUT DON'T THINK YOU'RE IN A LEAGUE BY YOURSELF. I PLAYED 18 HOLES ONCE AND SHOT 1,851.
>
> YOUR FAITHFUL FAN, JOHN CANDY.

19

M*A*S*H 4,
Calgary 2

The new record was a high point in a season so filled with highs and lows I couldn't begin to guess what would happen next.

Leading into the All-Star break, we were playing awful, hanging limp in fourth place. Something had to give. Rogie Vachon traded my good friend Bernie Nicholls to shuffle the line-up and try to find some new ways to win. It wasn't an easy time. Bernie was my best friend on the team. He and I are a lot alike. We played golf together, went to the track together. When rumors started about Bernie being on the trading block, I pleaded his case with Rogie, but it didn't matter.

That shows you how stupid the image was of my being assistant general manager. Some writers thought Bruce would come to me about trades before he'd go to Rogie. That's not the way it worked at all. Sometimes Bruce and Rogie would ask me about a player in a way like, "Can this guy play off the wing?" I mean, I've been in the league twelve years, I've played against a few people. But the rumors were getting out of hand. There was even talk among my teammates that they were afraid to mess up around me or I'd have them traded.

Rogie obviously didn't listen to me about Bernie, who was sent to the Rangers for Tomas Sandstrom and Tony Granato, two right wingers. As much as I hated it, the deal didn't surprise me. And the way it worked out was probably for the best. The Rangers got a great scorer and a new leader, and we got two twenty-five-year-old guys with scoring ability, speed, and some grit on defense.

Bernie was steamed. He felt that he'd played eight years when the Kings were going nowhere and now that it's going good, he gets dealt. He pretty much ripped everyone on the Kings' management on NBC at the All-Star game in January.

It was like his words were a hex on us. After the All-Star break, we played so bad they should have sent us all to New Haven. Allan Malamud of the *Los Angeles Times* started calling us "Queens" instead of Kings. About me, he said, "The way he's playing, his nickname ought to be downgraded to The Good One." Then he said Larry Robinson, whom we'd talked out of retirement, belonged in the Legends game at the All-Star break.

Our biggest problem was we couldn't get all our best players on the ice at the same time. Kelly Hrudey, our goaltender, missed most of the year with mononucleosis. Larry lost ten pounds with the flu and Tony and Tomas kept getting themselves busted up. The three of us — Tomas, Tony and myself — played on the same line for only one stretch of five games. During that time we scored thirty-nine points. That's almost eight a game. That set my mind at ease. In fact, I'm convinced that line can be as good as our great Edmonton line of me, Jari Kurri and Esa Tikkanen. Sandstrom's a European-style star like Jari. And Granato's real pesky like Tik, only more talented offensively.

One reason we lost Sandstrom for so long was because of those very Oilers. On March 1, the Oilers and the Kings got into the biggest fight in NHL history, at least if you go by penalties. It was one of the sorriest things I've ever seen and, unfortunately, typical of this league.

You could almost see it coming. The Oilers were coming off a bad loss to Calgary. We were sitting in the middle of a bad year. I'm not sure how it started, except that my old Oiler teammate Glenn Anderson was in the middle of it. He punched Sandstrom, leaving him with a broken bone in his face and a scratched cornea that kept him out for weeks. That started an all-out brawl, with our own Marty McSorley going berserk. Marty was and still is close friends with a lot of the Oilers, but you wouldn't have known it on that night. Look, when my buddy Mark Messier of the Oilers hits me, he hits hard. Same with Kevin Lowe. Same with Marty. We're the best of friends, but if I got traded tomorrow, he'd hit me hard.

And that's what he tried to do to the Oilers. I think he was trying to say something that night, and it was, "I'm not an Oiler anymore. I'm a King." And maybe I was trying to say the same thing, because even I got into it. I jumped Steve Smith to try to keep him from pounding Brian Benning. All in all, it was a night that bloodied the ice, set a record for penalty minutes (356), and didn't do much for my campaign to ban fighting.

We started to play better after that, but then I went down with a groin injury on March 17. I missed two games, came back against the Rangers only to have Alan Kerr smash me from behind into Ken Baumgartner, and wrench my back something awful. I never even saw Kerr. All I saw was Kenny going "Heads up!" It was a cheap shot, if you want to know the truth, but one that the referees seem to let guys get away with. In football, you can't clip somebody from behind. It's not only illegal, it's dangerous. I really hope that our Players Association will try to take some serious steps to ban it for good.

Anyway, I didn't play the rest of the regular season. And as we started our playoff series with the Stanley Cup defending champion Calgary Flames, it looked like I might not play a single game. I had never missed a playoff game in my entire career, but this looked inevitable. I was walking like a sixty-year-old man. My daughter, Paulina, thought I was joking around, but I wasn't. My back was spasming like crazy. I was getting treatment on it every day for an hour in the morning and again for an hour in the afternoon. I was a wreck. The team flew off to Calgary without Larry Robinson and me. Most of the sportswriters figured the Kings were in trouble. After all, we'd lost six of our last eight in the regular season.

But that's when the team played one of the greatest games in franchise history. They were behind 3–1 in the third period and came back to win 5–3. It was not only one of the the greatest comebacks in Kings history, but it meant miles more because they'd done it without two of the team leaders. Maybe we were the problem all along.

The Kings lost Game Two up there, which you would figure, and flew home. So here was Game Three and I still hadn't played a minute. There was no way I could play, but at the same time, there was no way I *couldn't* play. This was too important. I thought about what it would feel like not to play, and it felt worse than any pain my back could throw at me. I gave it a try. I don't know why, though, the way my luck was running. That same day Frankly Perfect — one of the horses I own with Bruce McNall — stepped in a hole and broke his ankle at Santa Anita, ending the career of a fine thoroughbred.

Any bending over I was going to do was from the waist down, but I got lucky early in the game. I got a rebound of a shot by our Super Rookie, Rob Blake — this guy is going to be a superstar, mark my words — fed it to Tomas and he scored. We took them into overtime before Tony won it with an amazing shorthanded goal. I can't remember an ice bag feeling any better than the one on my back that night.

We routed them in Game Four, 12–4, and our

line, Tomas, Tony and I, had 15 points. Then we flew up for Game Five in Calgary, where they routed us back. We still led 3–2.

We were playing like we cared, like a team that didn't care about anything but winning. We were finally healthy and were playing like it. I had total confidence that we would win Game Six in L.A.

With only four minutes left in that game, though, it looked bad. We were down 3–2. If we flew back to Calgary for Game Seven, we were gonna fry. We had to do it here and now. And that's when I lost the greatest faceoff of my life.

The Flames' Joel Otto outquicked me on the drop and tried to flick it backwards. It hit his own shin pads and sort of flopped in front of me. I might lose a faceoff once, but I'm not going to blow it twice if you give me a chance. I pounced on it and flicked it to Steve Duchesne, and he blew it past Mike Vernon to send us into overtime. "Is that luck or skill?" Otto said later. "I guess his skill brings luck." Nah, Joel. Luck.

That's when my friend Mike Krusher won it for us. Krusher is the kind of guy the club thinks about trading in February but who makes first-team All-Star in April. He comes up big in the important games and he did that night. In double overtime, in one of the tightest, most thrilling games I've ever been in, Krusher dove for the puck fifteen feet in front of the Calgary net and somehow flicked it over Mike Vernon's glove. I still have no idea how Krusher did it, considering that all 215 pounds of Brian Maclellan were laying on top of him the whole time.

It was the second straight year we'd knocked out the Stanley Cup champions in the first round, and it seemed to make the regular season melt away. My back started to feel a lot better.

Naturally, that's when we got our tails handed to us by the Oilers in four straight in the second round. It never bothered me for a minute. We barely had enough guys to suit up. We had nine guys hurt, including yours truly, who got sideswiped by Steve Smith in Game Three and reinjured the back. I never played again. For Game Four, we did not even have enough healthy players to dress a full team. You're not going to win a Pee Wee tournament with that kind of depth.

For a lot of people, I guess that blowout loss to the Oilers said something about our team and about me and about the trade and everything. Everybody figures the Kings have faded out now. They figure we had our chance my first year and did nothing with it. And, as I told you, they were saying we'll never win a Stanley Cup in Los Angeles and I'll never win another MVP.

All that talk is just a lot of hot air from people who want to create a controversy. It's like when people ask what I think about the Oilers winning the 1990 Stanley Cup and Mark Messier winning the Hart Trophy as MVP the same year. I guess they expect me to be jealous (there's that word again) or angry or regretful. But here's the truth. During the finals, I watched and was happy for the guys. I would have liked it to be my team lifting the Cup, but those guys were my second choice. And when Mark won the MVP at the NHL Awards show two weeks later, Janet and I were next to him the whole day, worrying for him. When he won, I swear, I was almost as excited as when I won in 1989. When he stepped up to the podium to receive his trophy, he cried, Janet cried and I cried. Other than that, we didn't care at all.

Look, when I broke down at that press conference announcing my trade to the Kings, I wasn't just feeling sadness at leaving my friends. I knew I was leaving future Stanley Cups behind. I'm sure that one won't be the last for them, either. They might win two more. There was a closeness on our teams there that I've never seen anywhere else in sports — and it's still there. Take Danny Gare. Danny is an old veteran and a great guy who played most of that year with the Oilers but was released by Slats just before the playoffs began. Most of the guys knew Danny would probably never be in hockey again, which meant that his last chance to win a Stanley Cup had just gone out the window. So what did the Oiler players do? They pitched in and bought him a plane ticket to the last game against Boston, got him back in the dressing room and, when they won it, made sure he took a long drink from the trophy. And that is what makes the Oilers win.

But sad as I was to leave I was excited by the new challenge of making hockey more popular in L.A. and the western United States, and of bringing the Kings a Stanley Cup. I know, I know. We haven't done it yet. But Rome wasn't built in a day. For that matter, neither was Edmonton. The Kings will have their day in the L.A. sun. Just watch us.

20

A Thank-You Note

I know exactly how I want to quit. I want my last game to be tied with ten seconds left and I help win it with an assist. Preferably, the puck would go in the goal after it bounces off Esa Tikkanen's rear end, but I'm not particular. Then I'll give the Stanley Cup one last spin, conduct my last press conference on this earth, drink my last locker room beer, go have dinner at my favorite restaurant in L.A., order the good stuff and raise a toast to a new life.

The new contract I signed in 1990 allows me to play nine more years if I want, which would make me thirty-nine. But if I can't play, I won't. I don't want anybody telling me when to retire. I know it's going to be tough. I just don't want to hang on past my welcome.

Not that it's going to happen anytime soon. In L.A., I feel refreshed. L.A. has extended my career probably four or five years. I love hockey now more than ever.

I get these dreams. I dream of holding up the Stanley Cup in the L.A. Forum. Probably my fondest memory is picking up the Stanley Cup the first time. As a kid, I watched all the great players pick up that Cup. To this day, I can still see Jean Beliveau of the Canadiens picking it up and holding it over his head. I must have rehearsed how I would do it ten thousand times. And when it came true on that May night in 1984, it was like an electric jolt up my spine.

People ask me about all the records I set. They mean a lot, obviously, but I know most of them will be broken. When Gordie set all his records, nobody figured they'd be broken and now they're saying the same thing about mine. Somebody will come along and break most of them and it might be Mario Lemieux. I think Mario could break any of my records, but fifty in thirty-nine is going to be the toughest. I think 200 points is easily possible and so is the fifty-one-straight scoring streak. He nearly did that already. I think Mario has the potential to write me out of a lot of records if his back heals up and he stops smoking. I know it's none of my business, but you can't smoke and stay as absolutely sharp as you need to be. Still, he's a pleasure to watch. About three weeks into the 89–90 season, he started a consecutive-points streak that looked unstoppable. By about the thirtieth game, I figured my streak of fifty-one was history. He wasn't just getting a point a game, he was getting three and four. But he suffered a herniated disk in his back somewhere in there and you could see it was killing him. Around game forty-two, my ex-Oiler teammate Paul Coffey, now with the Penguins, told me, "He's in a lot of pain, Gretz. I can't believe he's even out there."

I knew exactly what he was going through. Just watching him try to play made me wince for the torn shoulder I played with for the last nine games of my streak. The personal and media attention are hard enough when you're trying to break a record, but when your body wants to be lying in a swimming pool full of ice it's even tougher. Finally, after forty-six straight games, Mario played two periods against the New York Rangers and was in so much pain he couldn't come back to the ice. The streak was over.

You might not believe this, but I honestly didn't care if he broke it. For one thing, he's a great player and a friend. For another, my fifty-one would at least stand as the longest streak from opening day. Mike Barnett always reminds me that fifty-one shouldn't even be the record, by the way. I scored in nine straight games at the end of the season before that, making it sixty straight games. In any sport, baseball, basketball, whatever, streaks carry over. It's not like you failed or got shut out along the way. You didn't. You just ran out of season.

Hockey teaches you humility. I remember one summer I was in Toronto visiting the Hockey Hall of Fame. I love the Hockey Hall of Fame. I could be accidentally locked in there some night and I still wouldn't see everything I wanted to see. Anyway, I was standing there in front of a big picture of me and Gordie. All of a sudden someone tapped me on the back and said, sort of angrily, "Do you mind getting out of the way? I'm *trying* to take a picture of Gretzky and Howe."

I *am* proud of a few things. I've got the first, second, third, fourth, fifth, sixth and seventh best assist years in league history. I'm proud that I've either tied or led the league in assists every year I've played. You do that and your teammates tend to like you.

Besides, I'm not done yet. I'd like to be the first guy in history to get 2,000 assists. That would be about 850 more than anybody else. I think I can get 800 goals, too. That's exactly how many I'd like to finish with. Gordie has 801.

I'd love to play in the Olympics someday. I don't know how they could work it out with the NHL season, but if they could, I'd love it.

Speaking of wishes and lists, I've always wanted to do this and it's my book, so here goes. Here is my All-Star team of players I've played with and against. This is based not only on talent, but what they've done for the game, how much class they've shown and how tough they were in the clutch:

FIRST TEAM

Goalie	GRANT FUHR. Four Stanley Cups.
Defense	LARRY ROBINSON. Classiest man alive.
Defense	PAUL COFFEY. Can be as good on defense as anybody.
Forward	MARK MESSIER. Toughest competitor I ever knew.
Forward	MARIO LEMIEUX. Could end up as the greatest ever.
Forward	GORDIE HOWE. Not a bad front line, eh?

SECOND TEAM

Goalie	BILLY SMITH. Slashes or no slashes.
Defense	DENIS POTVIN. The real heart of the Islanders.
Defense	KEVIN LOWE. Courageous player.
Forward	JARI KURRI. The Finnish finisher.
Forward	STEVE YZERMAN. Quiet and classy.
Forward	GUY LAFLEUR. The Flower had flair.

Those guys changed the game. I think I have, too. I've changed the way people see the little guy. When I came up, it was always, "You're not big enough. They'll check you from here to next Thursday." But I think I showed that size isn't a factor. It's a finesse game, a speed game. And the sooner they outlaw this moronic fighting all the time, the faster it will get.

I also think I helped change the way people think of positions. Hockey isn't so much up and down the wings anymore. I think I've proven that what the textbook says is the right place to be is sometimes the worst place to be. You've got to keep moving, got to keep skating in and out of those pylons. I hope I've gotten rid of the idea that goals are everything in hockey. I hope kids think the assist is cool now, too, the way Magic and Bird made the pass cool again in basketball.

There's still a few marks on the game I'd like to make. I want to bring the Stanley Cup to Los Angeles. This is a city that has won every major championship trophy except that one. It deserves it. L.A. is the best sports city in the world. And if we can bring a Cup to L.A., think what that would do to the popularity of the game in America. I *know* hockey can be huge in the U.S. Every time Janet or I invites someone to see their first hockey game, they come away saying, "That was great! I love it!"

I can see some impact I've had in L.A. already. I was driving in Beverly Hills one day and came upon some kids playing roller hockey in the street. I was following my wife in her car and she rolled down her window and hollered, "Hey, guys! Look who's in the car behind me!" So I had to stop and sign something for everybody, but I loved it. Can you imagine? Roller hockey in Beverly Hills!

Not that everybody likes the new hockey craze. People who were into hockey before I came aren't too pleased. I had a guy come up to me and say,

"Thanks to you, Wayne, it costs more to go to the games now, it's harder to get ice time and the stores are all sold out of the good equipment."

Another dream is to be an owner of an NHL team. Unfortunately, it takes around $40 million, so, unless I win the lottery, it's out of the question. I know one thing, I don't want to coach and I don't want to be a general manager.

If I can't own an NHL team, I'd like to bring an NBA team to Toronto. I'm working with a bunch of investors on it. Toronto would eat it up and maybe I'd put myself in for a few minutes at point guard.

One thing I won't do is what everybody else wants to do when they retire — go fishing. I hate fishing. I can remember one of the very few times when I enjoyed a fishing trip. I'd won this limousine for being named Player of the Year. Winning a car or a limo sounds great until you win one. Through All-Star MVPs and Player of the Years and all, I think I've won thirteen cars. I've given them all away. Most of them I gave to my brothers and sister. And what was I going to do with a limo? Hire some guy to take me to the rink at night? So I wasn't too excited about this limo and it was just after the season, and right about then, my dad said he wanted to go fishing. So I said, "Fine, I'll go fishing, *if* we can fish my way."

The next morning, I pulled up in the limo along with Mike Barnett. My dad just stared at us. We headed out toward the lake, but instead of taking the normal road, we went the four-wheel route, banging through the brush and the woods and the

weeds. Finally, we came barreling out of the under-
brush, wheeled right up to the edge of the lake —
two of my tires were in the water — rolled down
the tinted window just enough and stuck the poles
out. We didn't get a bite and I, personally, couldn't
have cared less.

I plan on being Mr. Mom. I never told you how
Janet's pregnancy came out, did I? Well, this is the
Number 1 thrill of all time, period. On December
19, 1988, at 11:55 A.M., in Cedars-Sinai Hospital in
Los Angeles, one Paulina Mary Jean Gretzky was
born: twenty-one inches long, seven pounds, thirteen ounces. It was the same day we had our team
Christmas skate. I asked Janet if I could just take
her out on the ice real quick. I believe if she could
have gotten the I.V. out, she'd have strangled me.

I was there through the whole birth but I admit,
I choked. I got so nervous that for the first ten minutes, I couldn't even work my video camera. The
anesthesiologist did it for me. When we saw the
baby, we all were crying, Janet and me and Paulina, Janet and me mostly because she was perfectly
healthy, thank God. We've spent too much time
with Joey and Aunt Ellen not to think about it. I
was so pumped up, I slept that night in the chair
next to the bed and went to practice the next day
even more hunched over than usual.

Right after the birth, everybody came in to see
the baby — Janet's brother and mom and my
brothers and mom and friends and relatives. And
in the rush to see Paulina, everybody forgot about
Janet. Except Aunt Ellen. As soon as she walked in,
she ran up to Janet, who looked as tired as you

might think, and said, "Are you OK?"

I can't tell you how much Paulina looks like my grandmother Mary. Sadly, my grandma died a week before the birth. She had been unconscious for about ten days, but we had the ultrasound, so I was able to tell her it was a little girl before she died. Paulina makes the same kind of facial expressions. Unfortunately, she's just like my dad, too: If there are people around, she won't go to sleep. She also has one thing none of the rest of us have: dual citizenship.

Naturally, Paulina was a big deal in Canada. And it was made even bigger because we didn't want to release a picture of her until she got a few days older and got some of the wrinkles out. Of course, this caused people to go crazy trying to figure out why we wouldn't let anyone see a picture. One paper actually had the nerve to suggest I wasn't the father — I still can't believe this — by printing a rumor that the reason we weren't releasing a picture was because the baby was black.

Paulina is such a kick — I call her Magoo — that Janet and I have both decided we want four or five more and we haven't wasted our time. Our second child, a boy, Ty Robert, was born just a few days ago as this was written in July, 1990. I can't think of anything more fun than driving all of them around to ballet lessons, baseball practice, tennis tournaments, and yeah, maybe even a hockey game or two, but only if *they* choose it. Anybody know where I can get a good deal on a Blue Goose?

Anyway, like I said, I can always tell when the

clock is running out. Before it does, I want to get in a few words about people who don't get a lot said about them, like my Aunt Ellen. Growing up with her, I learned that the best way to deal with people with disabilities is to just be yourself. Thanks to her, I'm not the least bit uncomfortable with the disabled, which is one reason I always loved having Joey, the Oilers clubhouse boy, around. And it's why I think I'm pretty good at hospitals and homes for the disabled. People call up the club and say, "We've got five Down syndrome kids who would love to see the game," and the first person the club calls is me.

I think I learned that from my mom, too. For Mom, getting Aunt Ellen was exactly like getting another child. You pick up after her, discipline her, take her places. I remember one day, she was all excited because we had decided to pack her lunch for school. She talked about it the whole night before and then the next morning. She couldn't wait to carry her lunchbox and go to school and then sit down with everybody else and have lunch. So my mom put her on the bus and off she went. But when my mom stopped in on her at lunchtime, she was surprised to see that Aunt Ellen was sitting there with an empty lap while everybody else was eating.

"Why isn't Ellen eating her lunch?" Mom asked the supervisor.

"Oh, she ate it," said the supervisor. "On the way to school."

The problem is, unlike a child, she's never going to grow up. She's very good, but it tries my mom.

And yet every year when I send my parents two tickets for a vacation in Florida or Hawaii, they won't go. They stay with Aunt Ellen. My mom is like that, never caring one iota about herself.

When I think of Joey and Aunt Ellen, and even when I think of my brother Glen and his huge heart but unlucky feet, I can't help but think how blessed I've been. Yeah, I've worked hard — hard as anybody — but you don't have to tell me a lot of my talent was God-given. I know that. You don't have to tell me I'm lucky. I know I am, every time I look at Janet and Paulina. What they ought to call me is The Grateful One.

And I feel lucky, too, for some of the other people in my life — like the fans. I don't know of any athlete who has had more support than I have. I noticed every time you stood and it was a thrill every time. Every time you asked for an autograph, it made me feel like somebody.

Thanks to my teammates, old and new, Cup or no Cup. The sheer joy of playing hockey with friends like you has been wonderful. Sometimes I feel like half my life was spent trying to climb out from under celebration piles. But with me, it will never be the Cups or the records or the money or the trophies that matter. It has always been and always will be the *game*. And nobody played the game better than you guys.

Thanks to Mike, who is not only a great business manager but a great friend. I don't know where I'd be without you but I'd hate to go there and find out.

Thanks, Mom, for raising all five of us, putting

everything you needed on the back burner so we could have what we wanted. And then, when we were finally gone, you took on Aunt Ellen even though you knew it wouldn't be the easiest of tasks. I don't know if I could be that selfless.

Thanks, Dad. You taught me to play hockey, yes, but that wasn't the half of it. You taught me to be fair, to do the right thing, to respect people and, most of all, to be a man. Not that it was tough to learn. All I had to do was watch.

And, of course, thanks, Janet. By the time I retire, you'll have pretty much put your career on hold for eight years. You sacrificed that for me. I hope to return the favor. And you know, all the victories, records and good fortunes that have come my way to this point fall a distant second when compared to the two most precious gifts you've given me, Paulina Mary Jean and Ty Robert.

And they call *me* The Great Gretzky?

Wayne Gretzky's Lifetime Statistics

(*led league)

1976-77 Peterborough OHA

GP	G	A	PTS	PIM	Playoffs GP	G	A	PTS	PIM
3	0	3	3	0	—	—	—	—	—

1977-78 S.S. Marie OHA

GP	G	A	PTS	PIM	Playoffs GP	G	A	PTS	PIM
64	70	112	182	14	13	6	20	26	0

1978-79 Indianap./Edm. WHA

GP	G	A	PTS	PIM	Playoffs GP	G	A	PTS	PIM
8	3	3	6	0	—	—	—	—	—

1978-79 Edmonton WHA

GP	G	A	PTS	PIM	Playoffs GP	G	A	PTS	PIM
72	43	61	104	19	13	10*	10	20*	2

1979-80 Edmonton NHL

GP	G	A	PTS	PIM	Playoffs GP	G	A	PTS	PIM
79	51	86*	137*	21	3	2	1	3	0

1980-81 Edmonton NHL

GP	G	A	PTS	PIM	Playoffs GP	G	A	PTS	PIM
80	55	109*	164*	28	9	7	14	21	4

1981-82 Edmonton NHL

GP	G	A	PTS	PIM	Playoffs GP	G	A	PTS	PIM
80	92*	120*	212*	26	5	5	7	12	8

1982-83 Edmonton NHL

GP	G	A	PTS	PIM	Playoffs GP	G	A	PTS	PIM
80	71*	125*	196*	59	16	12	26*	38*	4

1983-84 Edmonton NHL

GP	G	A	PTS	PIM	Playoffs GP	G	A	PTS	PIM
74	87*	118*	205*	39	19	13	22*	35*	12